# STAGE 4

## Embracing A
## N.E.W.  S.T.A.R.T.

**Ydrate Nelson, M. Ed**

Ydrate Nelson/ BE THE GREATEST. Publishing

3101 N. Central Ave Suite 183 #760

Phoenix, Arizona 85004

Book Layout ©2022 Ydrate Creates Design/Ydrate The Motivator Nelson

Book Cover Design

Book Editor

—1st ed.

ISBN 978-0-9860929-4-7

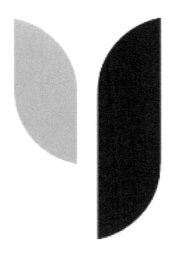

YDRATE NELSON

# CONTENTS

**Stage 1: The Journey Begins.** .......................................................1

In the Beginning. .......................................................1

The Cancer Treatment Center of America. .......................14

Next Level .......................................................17

**Stage 2: The Journey Begins** .......................................................22

Port and Liver Biopsy.......................................................22

The journey begins. Chemotherapy .......................................27

A Change is Coming .......................................................44

My wife and I… .......................................................47

**Stage 3: Charting A New Path** .......................................................50

Discovering Eden's Valley.......................................................50

Heading Home.......................................................73

Surgery Time .......................................................84

Waking Up From Surgery .......................................................87

**Stage 4: The N.E.W. S.T.A.R.T. Process** .......................................102

Embracing The Eight Laws of Health.......................................102

Nutrition.......................................................106

Exercise.......................................................121

Water.......................................................138

Sunshine .......................................................152

Temperance ......................................................................161

Air .....................................................................................173

Rest....................................................................................184

Trust In Self & God..........................................................194

**Conclusion** ....................................................................**204**

Scan the QR code and enjoy the narrated Flip Book version of Stage 4. Thanks for your support.

# Preface

Most people either know or know of someone who has suffered from the negative effects of a cancer diagnosis. We hear the stories and see the images online and on TV. As a result of the negative impressions, many people hear the word cancer and think the worst. They hear stage 4, and they think it's a death sentence. I was in that number. Then I was diagnosed. Most of the stage 4 patients I heard about prior to my diagnosis didn't have the most positive results.

To be completely honest, when heard I had stage 4 cancer, I didn't know if I would survive and live to write this book. I went to the doctor and got bad news five times in a row. At that point I just stopped looking at the information the doctors gave me as good or bad, I just prayed to God to give me the strength to handle whatever they brought my way. I was facing surgery, and the recommendation of chemotherapy along with a ton of questions that no one had the answers to. I was not willing to be presumptuous and think that I was so special that God would save me over all of the other people who prayed the same prayer that I had prayed. I had to face the reality that I could die and take my dreams to the grave right with me.

I knew that when Chadwick Boseman, the famed actor who introduced the world to Black Panther, was initially diagnosed, his status was stage 3 colon cancer. In my mind I thought, if he was a celebrity super star with more resources than I had, and it took him…it could take me too.

I wanted to live, and I felt that I could beat cancer but at the same time, I had to face the reality that I might not make it. I made up in my mind that I was not going to fear death. I was willing to accept that the will I had for my life might not be the will that God had for me. I do hold a certain level of fear when it comes to pain and extreme medical procedures, but I accepted death as an inevitable part of life.

I refused to live in fear. One day early on in my diagnosis, I had a realization. I thought to myself, if I am not afraid to die, why am I afraid to live? I decided to be more intentional about living my life and surviving. I wasn't willing to be comfortable with the possibility of death while fearing living a full life. I took every extreme action that I could to rid myself of cancer. This included extreme mindset and diet shifts, chemotherapy, along with surgery.

While recovering from surgery, I began to write when I could not sleep or get comfortable. Over the course of 4 weeks, I wrote this book based on my experience as I documented what I could remember about my cancer journey. This process was therapeutic for me, but my hope is that someone else will find it as a benefit for them as they fight one of life's many battles. My battle was a diagnosis called cancer.

Cancer is a very personal and individual battle. While there are some similarities, no two people or similar experience is the same. There are many variables and factors that go into the outcome of each patient. Everyone must be diligent and responsible for speaking up while finding what works best for them.

This is my personal experience and I own it, however, it is not meant to replace the recommendations of trained medical professionals. In my journey, I utilized a combination of traditional medication and surgery backed by a natural holistic approach. I was able to find a customized plan that worked uniquely for me. It is up to you and your team of advisors to find your perfect health and recovery plan. I wish you optimal mental and physical health on your quest to BE THE GREATEST that you can be.

## To my fellow cancer fighter, battlers, and survivors.

I want to take the time to send all my fellow cancer patients and survivors a special word. I want to encourage you to keep pushing and never give up. The battle is not easy, and you are not alone. There are millions of us in the battle daily. I know how hard it can be but remember why you are fighting. Don't forget your purpose or get distracted. You still have a mission. You are strong. You are capable. You are loved. You are not alone. You are more than a conquer.

**My Prayer for you:** I pray that God gives you the strength and tenacity to face the adversity and obstacles. I pray that your body is healing and getting stronger. I pray that you find peace with God's will for your life and know you have purpose and your life matters. I pray that your family has the strength to support and endure the days that might seem bleak. I pray that you embrace each day and be who God called you to be. You are Amazing. Blessings to you.

# Special Thank You.

Special thank you to The Cancer Treatment Center of America in Goodyear, Arizona and Eden Valley in Loveland, Colorado. Both organizations played a valuable lifesaving role in my recovery. I used the information from both organizations to find what worked for me and my body.

Each team of professionals gave me the best advice possible based on their professional knowledge and expertise. The dedication put forth by my medical and naturopathic team, were vital to my success. If it were not for the guidance from both teams, I can't guarantee that I would be here today. I am forever grateful for the roll they played in saving and preserving my life.

I would also like to thank the Jeremy Anderson Group and The Next Level Speakers Academy for their continued love, support, and most of all the many prayers I received over the course of this moment. The community has been instrumental in my journey and recovery. They showed up in one of the darkest seasons of my life and they continued to show up and I am truly grateful for those who invested in me.

A special thank you to all my family members (Nelson and Thomas) and friends who called and prayed for me consistently. I truly believe it was that love and support that helped me over come some of the darkest days and toughest battles of my life. I am truly grateful. Thank you all.

Finally, I have to thank my wife and kids, Dr. Kendra Stewart-Nelson, Eden, Noah, King and Zion. Fighting cancer is a family journey and I am grateful for mine. They motivated me to push through.

I am truly blessed to have the level of support I have been able to experience during my journey. It is hard to name all the people who were instrumental in my process, but God knows, and I pray their efforts will be mightily rewarded. I am thankful. I am blessed. God is good.

Keep the faith. Don't ever stop believing. Don't ever give up. You can do anything if you believe.

# STAGE 1

## *The Journey Begins.*

**In the Beginning.**
**Stage 4 - Embracing a NEWSTART.**

My name is Ydrate Nelson. I was born and raised in Dublin, Georgia to 2 teenage parents, Barbara Nelson, and Donald Thomas Sr. Since my parents had me at a young age out of wedlock, I spent a lot of time growing up with my maternal grandparents, Sammy, and Marion Nelson. From their house, I learned all the basic skills of life by observing my grandparents, aunts, uncles, and my mother. I was raised to be respectful to others no matter what, constantly saying, "Yes ma'am," and "No, sir" until this very day. I adopted this family value quickly, and if I ever slipped up, a reminder of how to conduct myself was always nearby.

I spent most of my childhood in a white, 6 room house full of family. In fact, during elementary school, there were 9 of us living in one house with 3 bedrooms. We didn't have a lot of money, but I never felt poor. I was blessed beyond measure because my entire family pitched in and made sure I was secure. I didn't spend one day hungry and there was nothing I wanted that my family didn't provide me with. My grandparents ensured

that we had food and shelter. From the outside looking in, it might have appeared that we that were not financially successful—or even financially stable, for that matter—but that never mattered because we had family wealth articulated by unconditional love and support.

My uncles, Nathaniel, Craig, and Sammy always looked out for me. They took me places shared experiences with me and help prepare me for the future. There was never a time in my youth when I didn't have father figures to look up to. I was blessed to have a family that stepped up to help and support me when I needed it most. My aunts, Bablin and Geneva, were like bonus moms in my life. They always made sure I was provided for and loved. Their support has been unwavering ever since I can remember.

I grew up close to my cousins and remain close to many of them today. They were some of my first friends and peer mentors. My cousins, Sanyo, and Bonita taught me about fashion and treated me like a little brother. My cousin, Latansey, was like my first little sister. I spent a great deal of time with my male cousins, Amanullah, Broderick, Maurice, Mangual Nelson (1973-2005), and Joel "Terry" Bell who we all called little Terry. My younger sisters, Renikko and Rashanda, were born when I was about 10 and 12 years old, respectively. By the time they reached middle school, I was already off to college. I missed a huge part of their life growing up, but I am proud of the ladies they have both become.

After graduating from West Laurens High School in 1996, I attended Valdosta State University, where I studied business and became a member of Alpha Phi Alpha fraternity incorporated. This is also where I met some of my closest friends, like Quentin Henry, Tremaine Neal, Charles Ferris Smith, Tyson Barrett, Mendez Hollis and many more. I was also blessed to have some of my childhood friends like Terrance Norris, Juan Wilson, Tapuwa Makaya, Charles Kinsey and Kelvin Davis in the city of Valdosta with me for years, so it always felt like home. I grew as a person in Valdosta and started my development as an independent man during my years there. I still have family there and will forever be connected to Valdosta. But after making it my home for 4 years, I relocated to Atlanta, Georgia to pursue my dream of being in the entertainment industry.

I lived with my team of KOHORTZ, Quentin Henry, Reggie Corbett, and Orenthal Kellam. We worked hard to manifest a successful music career. Even though we didn't reach superstardom in the entertainment industry, I developed great relationships and found success through other avenues.

After living in Atlanta for nearly 8 years, I decided to relocate to Phoenix, Arizona where my father lived. I established myself there quickly and was able to make myself at home., although I never intended on staying in Phoenix for long. Still, I felt it would give me a chance to experience a different perspective before returning to Atlanta where I would spend the remainder of my life.

So, I transferred my job from Atlanta to Phoenix and remained a top performer, which gave me an opportunity for advancement. I accepted a promotion with the understanding that I would remain in that position for at least a year. Fourteen years later and I still hold the same position at the same company. I have worked a variety of positions beyond the initial job that got me here—primarily in business, banking, and education. I embraced the journey of life and took on each challenge to the best of my ability.

Since relocating to Phoenix, I have been recognized with a variety of awards, all of which were a direct result of my dedication and hard work. I never set out with an intention to win an award; I simply focused on being an asset and adding value to those around me. Some of my noteworthy recognitions include the Bank of America Local Hero Award winner, Mitch Akin Mentor of the Year, P.A.L.S. Mentor of the year, 2019 Difference Maker Award Winner, 2020 Teacher of the Year (WPHS, Arizona), and the 2021 NLSA Perseverance Award, amongst others.

While I found success in a variety of areas, I had my share of adversity and issues from a haunting past. However, I established myself as a positive and motivated person to help me overcome inevitable hardships. I was diligent as I worked on the development of my mind for years. I went back to school for my master's degree and even became a certified life coach through the Southwest Institute of Healing Arts (SWIHA) to help both myself and others.

After years of loss while living in Georgia, I realized that staying motivated during adversity was both a journey and a process. In 2021, the years of hard work I put into my personal growth were finally put to the test.

I spent 4 years leading up to 2021 in the classroom as a high school teacher. I was the reigning teacher of the year and opted to take on more responsibility within the school. I was the head freshman football coach, teacher of marketing, digital media, digital communication, skills USA advisor, student advisor, and taught over 180 students each day.

I was so consumed in my job that I pushed through everything just to check things off my to-do list. I formed many bad habits as I consistently overwhelmed and over-worked myself. On top of my daily work responsibilities, I was a husband and father of 3. During this time, my wife and I found out that we were expecting our 4th child.

Since I led such a hectic and busy lifestyle, I fell behind on my personal health maintenance. I wasn't doing the simple things, like eating healthy and drinking enough water. My daily habits didn't support my desire to live a long, healthy, and productive life.

Over the course of a year, I started to notice changes in my body, but I didn't take immediate action. I was so busy that I put off the new symptoms I started experiencing. Instead of caring for myself, I cared for everything and everyone else, while I suffered from the inside out.

Being amid a pandemic at the time, I deemed my issues as minor compared to others who were suffering from Covid-19. And so, I decided to press on and keep quiet about the things I was experiencing. At the time, I was having strange gas, stomach pains, and cramps. I figured that it was a mixture of food related issues and just the consequences that came along with old age. But later, the pains started getting more intense, and I began to get nauseous every time I ate. Over the past few years, I had an abnormal amount of kidney stones and thought the pain could be related to that.

As the pain worsened, I went through a period of self-diagnosis. My father and I speculated on the possibilities as we re-visited our family's health history. We considered gallstones, kidney issues, and irritable bowel syndrome as possible culprits. But as we speculated, the pain continued to intensify.

I managed my illness and still performed well at my job. Most of the classes I taught were virtual, which gave me the flexibility I needed. After completing about 70% of the school year online, we were informed of our return to the classroom for the last 9 weeks of the school year. At this point, I grew a little concerned about managing my sickness in the classroom and decided that I would not eat at all when I was away from home. I ate one meal per day when I was in a safe space and could ensure privacy if needed.

By the end of the year, it was hard for me to eat many foods that I had been accustomed to eating. My stomach pains made eating unpleasant all together, and so, I decided to change my diet and began to eat even healthier. I ate more salads and plant-based foods but was still consuming some of the things I knew should have stayed away from.

So, I slowly eliminated these foods from my diet. The first to go was beef. I noticed how my body felt and responded when I ate it. The stomach pains grew sharper and more severe. I knew beef had to go, but I absolutely loved a good hamburger. I loved steak, ribs, spaghetti, lasagna, sausage, and beef hotdogs. Saying goodbye to beef meant saying goodbye to things I loved and had eaten my entire life.

While it was hard for me to walk away from beef on a mental level, the stomach pains made it that much easier. Whenever I wanted to eat something that was made of beef, I associated it with those stomach pains, which immediately removed any attractive qualities the food previously presented.

I still consumed a great deal of chicken and fish—primarily salmon. Fried chicken was a favorite. *Chic Fil A* and *Canes* were both less than a mile from my house and saw our family consistently. This made removing beef a little easier as well, since I wasn't only consuming plant-based foods.

When the school year came to an end, I planned on finally seeing a doctor, despite having put my health issues on hold for the entirety of the semester. As the yearbook advisor, I was focused on making sure I finished the job. I had students who were suffering through a pandemic and needed guidance. I had football players who needed mentoring over the term. I found a way to put my personal illness aside and focus on the mission at hand. But come summer, I finally got a chance to rest and relax. Over the first 2 weeks after the break, I started to really notice how my body was feeling. My pains seemed to be worsening, and at this point, they were accompanied by nausea and vomiting. I could not eat *Chic Fil A* or *Canes* without it all coming back up. I knew something was wrong.

When my wife saw how sick I was, she decided to contact a digestive specialist. The doctor recommended a colonoscopy and endoscopy to rule out certain illnesses and narrow down the root cause. I figured it was simply irritable bowel syndrome, but I wanted to look into each possibility.

## New beginnings

When I awoke from the procedure, I couldn't believe it was over. It seemed quick and painless. The doctor came in and started to go over the findings. He said they found a polyp and a tumor. "You will need to meet with a surgeon to get it removed and you might want to investigate additional forms of treatment," he said.

I grew confused and wasn't grasping what the doctor was telling me. "But what does that mean?" I asked.

"I'm sorry to be the one to break the news to you. You have colon cancer."

I still couldn't process what he was telling me or what it all meant. I simply got up, got dressed, and nodded as the nurses told me I'd receive a call the following day from the surgeon's office.

Feeling disassociated from the anesthesia and in shock from the news I had received, I headed toward my pregnant wife and 3 kids who were waiting for me in the car. "What did he say?" my wife asked.

Realizing that I'd have to say it out loud for the first time, I replied, "I have colon cancer."

This was the statement that set the foundation for my new reality.

It was time to embrace A N.E.W. S.T.A.R.T. and cultivate a motivated mindset.

The following day, the doctor's office called to let me know I was referred to a surgeon. A few hours later, I got the first call from the next doctor. At first, they told me they would see me in a few weeks because they hadn't yet received my file from the original doctor that diagnosed me. But once my file reached the new doctor, I was told the doctor wanted to see me urgently. At that point, I figured it was serious.

The following day, I got up and drove to the doctor's office. When I arrived, I had no idea what the conversation would be about. The doctor introduced himself and discussed the process of removing the cancer from my body. I still wasn't completely convinced that I had cancer. I asked the surgeon if he was sure surgery was required, and he stated that the biopsy was 90% accurate. He started to move fast and mapping out the process. I was still in disbelief as the doctor continued to explain. "The journey you are about to go through is not easy, but you will be a better person on the other side of it all," he said.

By the time I got home, I had received multiple calls from the hospital and different nurses who were preparing me for an operation. The one call that stuck out was a nurse who asked me about wearing a colostomy bag. I couldn't believe this is what my life was beginning to look like.

My wife was already working on the situation by the time I got home. She was contacting the Cancer Treatment Center of America (CTCA). They weren't convinced that I had cancer and weren't eager to take me in as a patient. After a consultation and meeting with several coordinators, I was set up for an appointment and evaluation. The people there who I first connected with were assuring and confident they could get to the bottom of my issue and get me back on track for a better life.

**The Cancer Treatment Center of America.**

When I initially went to the CTCA for my first appointment, I went alone. They ordered a scan of my entire body and ordered a copy of the results from the biopsy. I went in expecting the best and was hoping for a confirmation that I was not going to be coming to the center for long.

After I returned home, one of my friends asked me about my experience. I told her that I just had some blood work done, a scan, and a follow up with the doctor set up for later that week. She let me know that the doctor had likely already received the results from the tests they ran, and so, I tried to log into my patient portal to access the results.

At first, I had a hard time finding and understanding what I was reading. I scanned the image that confirmed they saw something in my colon and a few spots in my liver that looked suspicious. I was a nervous because I had to wait a few days before my follow up with the doctors to go over the results that I didn't quite understand through the portal on my own. I called my mother and father and told them what the doctors had all told me. They both assured me it would be fine and stated that it was common to have fatty tissue in and around the liver. They helped calm my nerves and told me to wait until my appointment.

On the day of the follow up, I met with my surgeon who was going to perform any surgeries I might need. She first confirmed that they had received the results from the biopsy, confirming that I had cancer. The hope I was holding onto suddenly faded. She also told me that it appeared to have spread to my liver, and I needed a biopsy on my liver, as well.

It hit me. I had cancer. I really had cancer.

As the doctor explained my likely path to survival, she discussed the options of chemotherapy and surgery. I could not believe what she was telling me. She grabbed a diagram of the human body to explain the process and procedure in more detail. At first, I recorded the conversation on my phone because I felt myself getting lightheaded. Within seconds, I passed out completely. When I awoke, all I could see was the bright and shiny light in my face. I thought I had died.

A few seconds later, my head went from leaning straight back and looking at the light in the ceiling to staring at the 6 medical professionals that were standing in front of me. They had me hooked up to several machines as they checked my body to ensure I wasn't having a heart attack. The doctors began talking to me, and I was just grateful to be alive. I was dazed and it took me a while to respond to the questions they were asking. "Call my father," I said as the doctor grabbed my phone and began dialing his number.

My father was already familiar with the CTCA because he was a patient at the same cancer center a year prior. In fact, I was diagnosed with cancer one day after my father's one-year anniversary of being cancer free. He was diagnosed with testicular cancer and had undergone treatment to rid his body of the cancer cells. The fact that he went through the process in the same facility gave me comfort and confidence in the staff and process.

When my father arrived, I still wasn't 100% back to reality. I was lightheaded, nauseous, and a bit confused. And so, the doctors set up a follow up appointment to continue the conversation and scheduled a liver biopsy, as well. I faced the possibility of chemotherapy and needed a port installed in my chest to have the chemo delivered into my body.

I went home that day with a different mindset. The reality of my situation was right before me, and now I had to figure out what to do to save my life. Life as I knew it was completely gone. Ready or not, I needed to fight if I wanted to live.

**Next Level**

Prior to the installation of my port for chemotherapy, I was given just enough time to take one trip to the Next Level Speakers Academy (NLSA) conference in Atlanta, Georgia. This was a vital part of my process to reinforce my mindset by surrounding myself with professional speakers for 3 days. I flew into Atlanta and stayed downtown at the Hilton Hotel for 5 days. While I was there, I met some of the most amazing people from around the world. Our leader, Jeremy Anderson, put together a community that became a vital part of my cancer journey.

While I was in Atlanta, I had the opportunity to connect with my friends and family. I had quite a few people stop by and visit while I was staying in my downtown accommodations. I received love and support from many of the people I held near and dear to my heart. I was grateful the conference allowed me the space and opportunity to give and receive the love I needed. It was a perfect way to kick off my treatment program.

While attending the conference, I had the opportunity to hear from some of the best speakers and leaders in my industry. I was inspired by the opportunity to be in the room with people who were living the life I dreamed of. It made me strong enough to grasp the reality I was living, and it helped me grasp the notion that this was something I could push through.

The second day of the conference, Dr. Tyrone Douglas gave a very emotional and spiritually connected presentation. At the end of his talk, the energy turned from a professional environment into something that felt more like church or a spiritual retreat. Everyone in the room were on their feet, and we all connected to the spirit of the Most High.

As I stood in my spot reflecting on my current situation, the leader of the Next Level Speaking Academy, Jeremy Anderson, came and led me to the front of the room. As I stood there, I felt hands being placed all over my body. Over 300 people prayed for me. It was the first time I cried in front of hundreds of people. We were all overtaken by the spirit of the room and many people shared in my emotions. This experience alone was worth the entire trip.

On the third day of the conference, to my surprise, I won the Next Level Speaker's Academy Perseverance Award. I had the opportunity to connect with the speakers and fellow audience members. The love and respect they showed me was exactly what I needed to return home and fight the battle of my life. For every person that didn't show up when I thought they would, I was blessed with multiple from the NLSA family that showed me nothing but genuine love and support.

These connections set me up for success as I returned home to face my journey.

Long after the emotions and excitement of the conference was over, many of the people I met became a vital part of my healing circle. I was able to secure several mentors and peers who were all on the same page that I was on. Few days passed without hearing from someone from that community. I am forever grateful for all that I've been given from the Next Level Speaking Academy.

# STAGE 2

# *The Journey Begins*

## Port and Liver Biopsy

As soon as I returned home from my trip, I knew it was time for my process to begin. The first procedure I underwent at the cancer center was having a port installed in my chest so I could receive chemotherapy, medicines, and labs. While the doctors installed the port into my chest, I also had a biopsy of the lesions on my liver to confirm whether it was really cancer.

On the day of the procedure, I had to be at the center at 5:30 AM for a COVID-19 test. Afterward, I was directed into a room for surgery prep. The staff made me incredibly comfortable even though I was not looking forward to the experience.

This was the first official surgical procedure of my life. I was unsure about the entire process, but I trusted God and the staff. I knew the consequences of not going through with the procedure and knew I could not play with my life.

I was directed into a medical room and instructed to go through the surgical prep process. I took off all my clothes and put on the gown and the comfortable socks they gave. The nurses came in and began the routine they'd clearly gone through so many times before me. While they prepped me, one of the nurses kindly described the details to me about the port I was going to receive. She asked if I wanted to see it. A part of me wanted to shut my eyes tight, while another part of me wanted to peel them open so as not to miss anything. When I finally nodded in agreement, she pulled it out and I stared in shock. "That's going in my chest and neck?" I asked. At that point, I just laid back and started to breathe my way through it all. It was overwhelming and I wasn't sure how to handle any of it.

I had a team of medical professionals who all came into the room to explain their role and reassure me I would be taken care of. I was ready to get the process over with. I was rolled away into another room where the procedure was going to take place and remember the anesthesiologist telling me I was about to take a nap. Within seconds, I was out.

I woke up in the recovery room, dazed and confused. The process was over, and I didn't feel a thing. I only had 2 bandages, one on my liver and a patch over the port installation. Everything went according to plan and most importantly, I woke up. The next step was to heal from the procedure and get ready for chemotherapy that started about 2 weeks later.

Prior to the start of chemotherapy, I had a meeting with my oncologist, the person in charge of overseeing my process and the surgeon. I went in, got my vitals taken like always, and waited for my follow up appointments. I met with the surgeon first. She entered the room and picked up with the conversation we previously had—the one we were in the middle of before I fainted. She started to again explain the surgical process the doctors and staff had to go through to remove the cancer from my body. This time, I was more prepared for the conversation and handled the information a lot better. I did not pass out. It was this day that I heard the doctors confirm and say something I never heard before: "We received the liver biopsy, and it came back positive for cancer, indicating that it has already spread. That means you are classified as stage 4."

I didn't flinch. I already knew it spread to my liver, but I wasn't sure of how the classifications worked. When she said stage 4, it didn't impact me in the way I would have thought because she didn't reveal anything new, except for the official classification title. When I went home, I had to do more research to find out what constitutes each class and what it really meant. I truthfully thought I was stage 1 but, in my ignorance, I didn't even know what that meant, either.

I needed clarity, so, I asked the doctor to explain the stages of cancer. She confirmed that stage 0 meant they had identified abnormal cells that have the potential to turn into cancer. Stage 1 meant that cancer formed in the innermost layer of the colon and may have spread to the muscle layer of the colon wall. Stage 2 meant that the cancer spread through the outermost layer of the colon wall to the tissue lining the organs in the abdomen. Stage 3 meant that cancer spread to the muscle layer or to the outermost layer of the colon wall and to nearby lymph nodes. Stage 4 meant that the cancer spread to one area or an organ that isn't near the colon. In my case, it was the liver.

As I started to understand what the stages meant, stage 4 didn't feel like a death sentence. If I didn't look at the portal before and read the chart before the doctors' conversation, I would have probably passed out again. But I already knew what the report said, I just didn't know how the classifications worked. I knew that even though I had a better understanding of the staging, when other people heard stage 4, they would think of death. In fact, prior to seeking further understanding, I thought the same thing.

After meeting with my surgeon, I met with my oncologist who went over the process and made sure I was aware of any possible side effects. This was my last visit before chemo started. I was very curious but didn't want to know too much because I didn't want to get into my own head. I was as ready as I was going to get. I wanted to live, and I was willing to do whatever it took to survive.

## The journey begins. Chemotherapy

I was not looking forward to chemotherapy at all. I spent the following 2 weeks after my procedures preparing my mind for the process. Everybody I talked to seemed to have a different experience and reacted differently from the chemotherapy. I knew that my process was going to be unique. The anticipation was torturous.

The night before my first chemotherapy session was nerve-wracking, to say the least. I spent far too much time researching the process of chemotherapy, landing myself deeper and deeper into the depths of my own mind with each scroll and click. I needed an outlet, so, I went back to my old method. I started to writing poetry and music like I did when I was twenty years younger. In the midst of writing, I managed to create a song called *God Has* that helped me process what I was going through. I wrote and recorded on my iPhone and then fell asleep.

The next morning, I woke up with a full agenda. I was scheduled to be at the CTCA at 9 in the morning to begin the process. I had no idea what to expect. I didn't know how I would feel mentally or physically. I checked in and got my agenda for the day. I went next door to the medical clinic to begin the process. I first had to see the nurses to get my labs and bloodwork before having my consult with the doctors.

As I sat there, I noticed all the people in the room. As a newcomer, I was a bit anxious. I observed a range of emotions glued on the faces of the people who sat patiently and waited as I did until we were all called back one by one.

There was an elderly couple who were already sitting in the waiting room before I got there. A nurse came into the waiting room and called the husband back to get his vitals drawn. As soon as he walked with the nurse, I noticed the lady next to him begin to cry. She got up and left. Vicariously, I felt the toll the situation was taking on her emotions. I felt a strong urge to cry, as well, and realized that I was sharing the same experience with so many others.

Finally, they called my name, and I was led to a room in the back. It started out with getting my bloodwork and vitals. This was the first time that I would be using the newly installed port. I was instructed to lift my shirt so the nurse could access the port. I felt a poke in my chest as the nurse attached the needle to my port that would be use for my vitals first and then to administer chemotherapy later in the day. A big bandage was placed over my port to keep the tube that was attached to the needle in place.

About an hour after taking my vitals, it was time to meet with my oncologist and begin chemo for the first time. She went over my results and cleared me to get started. I was then instructed to head to the infusion room for injections. I wasn't looking forward to the process, but I was ready for whatever was coming my way.

I went upstairs and checked in with the receptionist. She got me checked in and a few minutes later, a nurse came to get me and direct me back to my own personal chemotherapy bay. I had been anticipating this day for quite some time and it was finally here. I took my seat, took a few deep breaths, and prepared myself to step into the unknown.

They lifted my shirt and connected the chemotherapy tube right to the port in my upper chest. I was instructed to relax as the fluid started pumping through my body. The initial process was about 5 hours long as I sat there trying to sort through the emotions that were swirling inside me. Was my energy lower, or was it psychological? Did I need to rest, or did I need to push through? I was completely confused about my body and mental response to everything that I was facing at that moment.

My father sat next to me that day. I tried to entertain my mind by listening to music and scrolling through my phone and iPad. I also tried to nap through the process as much as possible, but all I could think about was the chemical being injected into my body. When it was finally over 5 hours later, I realized it wasn't really over. In fact, it had only just begun.

The nurse who administered the chemo came in and told me that the infusion was over, and it was time to be disconnected from the IV infusion. As I was being connected from one tube, I had no idea there was a take home pump that would be running from my chest to a pack that I would wear around my waist for an additional 46 hours. I could not take the bag off and would have to do everything with this pump for the following 2 days. I was shocked because as I was being connected to this pump, it was the first time I had ever even seen this type of equipment and now it was part of my life.

I had to use the restroom and take a bath with this machine still connected to a tube in my chest. Every few minutes or so, I would hear the pump scream, indicating that my body was being injected with the chemotherapy medicine. This went on for 46 straight hours.

Sleeping was a challenge as I had to figure out the best way to sleep without unplugging the tube from my chest. I slept sitting almost upward on the couch because I was so worried that one small movement would make something go terribly wrong. The doctors told me that disconnecting the tube would constitute an emergency. So, I tried my best, tossing and turning ever so carefully, sleeping, bathing, and living with this tube in my chest.

I was very cautious the entire time and monitored my mental and physical energy. After 2 days of wearing the chemo bag on my hip, it was time to return to the Cancer Center for my disconnection. When I got there, I had to receive additional fluids and sit in the chemo bay for another hour and a half. I had a chance to observe other people again and their support systems as they went through the same thing I was. I knew that there were others who felt the exact same way I did, and although I felt lonely at times, I knew there was a sea of people fighting to live, just like me.

After I was disconnected from the chemo bag and all the tubes, I felt free. I was warned about some potential side effects, though, that ranged from a change in energy, thinning of hair, different pains, nausea, neuropathy, and so on. I felt fine while the doctor ran through this list with me, and so, I thought I was in the clear from the side effects she was listing. But that changed rather quickly.

As soon as I was finished, I went straight to the bathroom. My body was full of liquid and I needed to release it all. While I washed my hands, I noticed my fingers tingling and knew my hands, as if there was no blood circulating through my veins. I let the nurse know on my way out of the bathroom, and he assured me that it would go away in a few days. He warned me about the cold sensitivity and urged me to be aware of all the possibilities that come along with chemo, but it was nothing to worry about. He gave me a heating pad and I was on my way home. When I arrived, the severe back pain kicked in and my energy levels bottomed out.

The next morning, I had to deliver a virtual speech for work. But I woke up feeling like a zombie. My brain felt sluggish and I was trying hard to push myself mentally, but I was completely drained physically. I could barely stay awake and felt my entire body crashing. I pushed through the presentation regardless—thought I'm sure it as obvious—and let myself rest for hours after. My body was burned out and I had no choice but to rest.

It took me a few days to get back on track. I was trapped between pushing harder and resting appropriately. I got the pump off on Friday and it took me until Monday to get my energy levels back to about 80%. As my energy levels returned, I noticed my cold sensitivity increasing. On Monday morning, as I was fixing my kids cereal for breakfast, my hands went numb while pouring milk. I figured it would take a few more days for the symptoms to go away, but I visited the grocery store later and grabbed cold items when I noticed my hands go completely numb. I had to use my shirt to put cold items on the conveyor belt.

Over the next few days, I noticed the cold sensitivity was still intense. I ordered some compression gloves and socks and wore them daily up until my next chemo session.

The first time I drank something cold and had a severe response was incredibly frightening. I poured some juice into a cup from the refrigerator and when I swallowed the juice, it felt as if my throat was going closing and as if I was pouring pins and needles into my mouth. I was warned about the side effects but was startled and concerned nonetheless.

My chemotherapy session was scheduled for every 2 weeks. I was scheduled for August 18th, one day before the scheduled C-section for my 4th child and my son, King's, second birthday. When I thought of the fact that my kids were going to share the same birthday, I knew I had to push myself like never before.

I wasn't looking forward to my second chemotherapy infusion. I went with mixed emotions. I knew my life was on the line and I had to do something but at the same time, I wasn't coping well with the side effects of it all.

When I arrived at the Cancer Center, I checked in and went to the clinic to get my vitals and blood work taken. Next, I met with my team of doctors to go over my bloodwork once more to establish a game plan for the day. As the doctors reviewed my results, they noticed that my white blood count was cut in half after the first chemotherapy session. I also let them know that the numbness that I thought would go away after a few days was still there. Still, they assured me that I was okay to move forward, and so went on with the scheduled session of chemo.

I went upstairs to the infusion center and checked in. My nurse came and got me from the waiting room and took me to my infusion bay. I was scheduled for 5 hours of infusion, plus the chemotherapy bag for another 46 hours. I then had to return to the infusion center 2 days later, receive an additional hour of infusion, then get disconnected. It was a total of 51 hours of straight infusions. I began preparing my mind for the journey.

During chemo, I usually found a soundtrack or some music that helped me zone my mental thoughts. I also started to write and record my own music, which allowed me to benefit from the creative process at home and gave me something to listen to inspire myself to keep moving forward. As I worked to get my soundtrack and entertainment hooked up for the 5-hour infusion, my nurse began hooking me up to the machines and the process was officially underway.

As I sat in the chair and received my infusion, I pulled up the bloodwork results from my labs in my patient portal. The doctors updated all the labs, imaging, and reports inside the portal, and I learned how to read and obtain the information. According to the conversation with my doctors earlier, I realized that even though I had cancer in my liver and colon, neither of them were a threat to my life. As the nurse who was taking care of me while being infused came by to check on me,

I asked him to look at my bloodwork and see if he could answer a few questions that were lingering in my mind.

He said that my liver function was good and the other areas that were abnormal were all correctable. I then asked him a question that had been plaguing my mind for a while, "What is the biggest threat to my life?" Based on what he could see, he said the biggest threats were from infections because my white blood count was low and I had blood clots. I asked if either of these things had anything to do with cancer directly, and he shook his head. At that moment, I realized that the biggest threat to my life was a result of the treatment and not my cancer diagnosis.

At that point, I knew I had to find a way to help build my body up in the areas where chemotherapy was breaking it down. To pass the time, I left my music and writing to the side, and started searching for ways to improve the deficiencies in my body instead. I looked for every natural solution I could find. My mind was focused on rehabilitating my body and building it up to be as strong as I possibly could.

When I left the Cancer Center that day, I headed home to rest for the big day. King was turning 2 and my son, Zion, was going to be born. I went home and dealt with a ton of adversity as we prepared for the 6:00 am check in at the hospital. COVID-19 restrictions were in place and visitors were limited, so, it was going to be just my wife and I.

As I laid down the night before, the reality of my situation played on a screen before my eyes as I maneuvered the chemo bag that was attached to my hip. The sound of the bag was consistent and it acted as a reminder that I was being treated for cancer. For 46 hours straight, the sound and reality of the chemo process was unescapable, and I grew to despise the sound it made.

I did not rest very well the day prior to my son being born because I was afraid that I was going to oversleep and the discomfort of having the chemo pump on my hip deterred me from any form of rest. My wife and I woke up the next morning and went to the hospital for our check-in time. I was in the middle of my chemo cycle and the process had me physically and mentally drained. But regardless of how I felt, I knew I had to show up for my family.

We went through the sign in and registration process and went into the room to get prepared for the process. My wife got changed into her gown and I put on my protective coverings. They took my wife back first, and I sat in the waiting room as they prepared for the procedure. As I sat there, I only heard 2 sounds. I heard the thud of the ventilation system and the sound of the chemotherapy pump administering the medicine into my body. This was my 4th time sitting in this room, but this time felt different.

After about twenty minutes, a nurse came back and took me into a room where my wife was prepped and ready to deliver our 4th child. I sat next to her and adjusted my chemo bag. As the doctors pulled my son out of my wife, I heard my son cry for the first time, and it drowned out the sound of the chemotherapy bag pumping both life and death in me.

That night was a challenge. I was already tired from the night before, and now I had a newborn to take care of while my wife recovered. I got very little sleep. I had the chemo pump on my hip and a newborn baby on my lap. I was on my last mental and physical leg.

The next day, I had to leave my wife and newborn son at the hospital and return to the CTCA to have the chemo pump removed. I had to go through the hour-long infusion process and then finally get disconnected from the pump. 51 hours were over. Like last time, I headed into the restroom to relieve myself. When I washed my hands, they went completely numb and blue, and the tingling was more severe than the previous time. I started to panic. I could hardly open the restroom door. When I did, I screamed to the nurse for help. "I can't feel my hands," I said urgently as one nurse called over another to look at my hands. They rushed me to a sink and started running hot water over my fingers. After a few minutes, the feeling started to return, and I was able to move my fingers.

The nurse gave me a heat pack for my hands, and I put on my hoodie and went back to the hospital to be with my wife and son. I was drained and could barely walk. The COVID-19 restrictions only allowed one visitor so, I couldn't even have someone take my place at the hospital. I was more tired than I could even remember, but I know I was mentally struggling to push myself through the physical toll that was being taken on my body.

That night was one of the hardest nights of my life. After being in chemotherapy for 51 hours straight, my body experienced an extreme crash but I had to force myself to stay awake to take care of my son. As I sat in that chair in the hospital trying my best not to drop him, I knew I had to make a change and try something different with my treatment program.

The following day, it was time to get ready to go home. My energy levels were still incredibly low, and my feet were dragging across the white floors. I was in a zombie state. I headed to go to the car to grab the car seat so the nurse could ensure the baby was properly strapped in. When I got to the car, I had to take a break just from the short walk from the room to the parking lot. I opened the back seat of the family minivan and unbuckled the car seat and started my journey back to the room, exhausted.

My fingers were turning numb and blue while I held the seat. I stopped periodically to rotate my hands and grew increasingly worried about my ability to help take care of my family. It took me way longer than normal to make it back to the room. When I got there, I felt as if I could not take another step. I felt trapped inside my body. I could barely even respond when my wife asked me what I had plopped myself into a chair. I was officially crashing.

With the help of the medical staff and the healthcare professionals, we were able to get packed up and ready to transition from the hospital to home. I was tired. I couldn't even drive my wife and newborn kid home because I was afraid I would pass out behind the wheel. At that point, my appetite was completely suppressed, and I had not eaten in days. I asked Ricardo, my designated driver, to stop by *Chic Fil A*, even though I had not eaten meat in a while because of my required diet changes. I ate the sandwich, the fries, and drank my Arnold Palmer. When I got home, my wife and I realized we were in a vulnerable position. Luckily, we had a day or so to prepare before our other 3 kids returned home. My wife had just had a major procedure to birth our child. I was one day removed from chemo and on a downward energy crash, and we had a newborn that had to be taken care of. Even though I was already dealing with minimum sleep, I didn't anticipate much in my near future.

I struggled through the night to help my wife and take care of our new son. I don't know how I did it, but we made it happen. The next day, our other kids, Eden 8, Noah 6, and King 2, returned home. I was happy to have them back, but I knew that it was a new level of struggle we had to experience together as a family. It was hard on our kids, too. As a father and husband, I felt a level of stress like never before. Life couldn't have been more real than it was at that moment.

The first night having the kids' home wasn't as bad as we expected. Our daughter, Eden, was helpful, and our son, Noah, spent time with our 2-year-old. We found a way to support each other as a family. We all grew, and I saw my kids step up to the plate and mature as human beings. I saw their compassion, understanding, and work ethic begin to grow. I knew that something good was going to come out of this situation.

I keep getting stronger by the day, but it was taking me longer to recover than the first time. I found myself pushing my body to its maximum potential. I was also dealing with neuropathy and my hands were still very sensitive to the cold. My toes tingled when I walked. I was still looking at over 500 more hours of chemotherapy and I didn't think I would be able to sustain myself through much. I was feeling my body go through ups and down and was getting weaker each time I got an infusion. So, I had a decision to make.

## A Change is Coming

The 2 weeks leading into my next chemo session were very reflective for me. I was now dealing with the side effects from the treatment, was trying to be a husband, and was a father of 4 young children. I went back and forth about what I should do. One day, I was on a call with my dear friend, Steven 'Big Nebs' Goard, and he gave some advice that changed my entire approach to how I facilitated my treatment program. He said, "Before you listen to somebody, listen to your body." This became the foundation of my mindset. If I had taken this advice earlier, I might not have been in the situation I found myself in earlier. I ignored the warning signs and kept pushing but that was no longer working in my favor. This time, I was going to listen to my body.

Over the course of the next few weeks leading into my chemo treatment, I paid close attention to my bloodwork readings from my patient portal, my diet, and the actions I needed to take to survive. When I looked at my bloodwork, I focused on all the things that were abnormally high and low. I then researched every natural option to help build my body back into shape. Although this was something I was already doing before, I became obsessed with getting rid of the red marks on my report. I became a student of natural medicine and remedies. I spent hours and thousands of dollars trying different diets, vitamins, and natural medicines. I was particularly invested in my white blood cell count and my vitamin D levels which was at an 8 and should have been at a 75 based on my doctors recommendation. I also focused on my glucose levels among other things because I was given a pre-diabetic status earlier in the year.

I changed my diet and cut out meat and sugar entirely. I went on a vegan fast and started walking every day. I was searching for an alternative to my current treatment and knew that doing nothing was not an option. I started to look further into people who had beat cancer using natural remedies and created my treatment plan on my own. I went back and forth with the idea of pausing my chemotherapy and trying my own plan, or just sticking it out and putting my life completely in the doctors' hands.

This was one of the biggest decisions of my life because survival was on the line. I knew that the process I was going through needed to be customized for me based on what my body was telling me. I spoke with 4 different people who experienced a variety of different types of cancers. Our treatment programs were very similar even though our situations were different. I wanted to find something more concentrated and tailored to my situation. I continued to do research and consult with my support system. I felt it was time for a new approach to the situation. The goal was to survive. The longer I was off chemo, the stronger my body got. In my mind, I had already told myself I was going to stop chemotherapy, but I had not shared it with anyone because I knew it would come with mixed emotions.

Even before I shared my decision to pause chemotherapy, I started to get a lot of different confirmations. People sent me natural options and ways to help build my body back up. I started gaining confidence in my ability to create a strategic plan to beat cancer. I sought mentors and information to help me create a plan. I ordered books and solicited information. I wanted to make an informed decision.

**My wife and I...**

When I first explained to my wife my line of thinking, she appeared to be on board. I explained my desire to pause chemotherapy and some additional options into which I was looking. She understood where I was coming from, but also wanted me to continue with chemotherapy because she felt it was the most effective treatment based on my experiences thus far. Her mother and sister both survived cancer and chemotherapy worked for them, so she felt it would work for me, too.

We agreed to pause chemo, which she assumed was a short-term and temporary method of action. When we went to the CTCA, they drew my blood, took my vitals, and set up for me to be infused. I informed the doctors I would be pausing my chemotherapy for a while and that this was going to be my last infusion. The doctors seemed concerned and advised me that I was making a mistake. I told them I was looking into other options to help build my body back up in the areas that chemo was breaking it down, and they reluctantly agreed that it might help my body to get some needed rest.

Shortly after stopping, my wife started thinking it was time to return to chemo. But I still wasn't convinced, which led to tension between my wife and I. We stopped seeing eye-to-eye and started experiencing riffs in our relationship. I felt as though she wasn't being supportive, and she felt as though she wasn't being heard. In her eyes, I was making a mistake because she didn't know anyone who had used alternative methods to beat cancer. I understood her concern and fears, but I was going into uncharted territory, standing on faith and doing what I felt needed to be done.

While I respected the medical advice and all the advances that have been made in cancer research, I still felt it was a very personal decision and experience. While other people offered their advice, it was still my body and mind that were being impacted. Despite what anyone one else thought, I needed to take my treatment program to another level to advance my progress and prove that I had what it took to beat cancer using alternative methods based on what my body was telling me. This was a very tense time in my medical journey and my marriage. I took a leap of faith and put my marriage and my life on the line to do it. It was all or nothing.

I did not know if I was going to live or die. I put my life on the line and took control of my own destiny. At this point, I was more concerned with the quality of life I was living than dying. I wasn't afraid of death. I was afraid of living a miserable life.

# STAGE 3

# *Charting A New Path*

### Discovering Eden's Valley

While I was searching for alternative methods to replace or aid the treatment program from the CTCA, one of my mentors suggested trying a naturopathic cancer treatment program in Colorado. Little did I know that this suggestion was about to change the direction of my entire treatment journey. He described a similar program he went through in Georgia and some of the activities he was involved in. He explained that the one in Colorado had an even more concentrated program that might be a good fit for what I was looking for. It was called *Eden's Valley*. I immediately felt a connection to the program, especially since my daughter's name is Eden.

Before calling, I visited the organization's website and did my research. The natural approach and trained team were available to help aid me in my journey. From the initial call, I felt as if I found an answer to a prayer.

The first day I called was on a Friday, but no one answered. I started to question and doubt the decision. I thought it might have been a sign. I called the same spot my mentor went to in Georgia, and they answered. I spoke with them about what they had to offer. It wasn't as intense as the Colorado program and a fraction of the cost. Looking to make a quick move, I paid the deposit right then and there.

I wanted to check into the Colorado organization as another part of my treatment program because it was closer to home in Arizona. On Monday, I called, and someone answered right away. Gina, the lady who answered my call, understood exactly what I was looking for. She informed me that the next available program was a few months away. I told her that I was going to a program in Georgia and that would cover the gap until I could get there. Before we hung up, Gina asked, "Do you mind if I pray for you?"

I couldn't believe it. "By all means," I replied, touched, and filled with warmth. She prayed a genuine and sincere prayer, and I knew Eden's Valley was the place for my treatment. I just had to be patient.

A few days later, I was in the recording studio working on some music when I received a call from Eden's Valley. They informed me that they had an opening in the program that started in a week. She asked if I would be interested. Even though I had already paid the deposit for the other program, I immediately agreed. She gave me the details on how to complete the registration process and pay the deposit. Within minutes, I was in the program. I went online and booked a flight. Even though I was flying in a week, I found a round trip flight from Phoenix to Denver for $72. I knew it was meant to be.

At that point, I felt like I had my alternative to chemotherapy and explained my plan to my wife. She was still leaning more toward the idea of chemo as a treatment, and it led to a conflict between us. Still, I knew I had to move forward with what I thought was best for me and my health. When my wife realized I was serious and was going through with the treatment despite her stance, she started offering more support for my decision.

My wife and kids dropped me off at the airport and I was on my way to Denver.

Sunday, September 5th.

8:43 Land at Denver airport

When I landed in Denver, Eden's Valley had a driver sent to pick up the people for the program. The compound was about an hour outside of Denver, so, having a ride available was a huge relief. When I landed and got off the plane, I called my driver, Joe. He met me and informed me that I was the first to arrive and we were still waiting on 5 others. They were coming from different places and landing at different times. Joe and I spent time together and got familiar with one another.

After about an hour or 2, everyone landed and we packed into the passenger van to begin our trip to Loveland, Colorado. I had no idea what to expect. Joe was amazing and the people in the van were just like me. We didn't know how this experience was going to go or what to expect, but we were in it together, and that somehow brought relief.

When we arrived at Eden's Valley, I could feel the peace overtake my tired body. We saw acres of land stretched before us, with a collection of homes and buildings spread out all around. It was a community. Each person or couple in the van were assigned their own room. We were spread out between 2 different houses on the compound. I was assigned to room number 7 in the back. I had a water bottle with my name on it, a journal for notes, and an itinerary for the next 2 weeks.

12:36 PM Arrive at Eden's Valley

When I first arrived at Eden's Valley in Colorado, I saw the huge letters outside one of the main facilities printed: NEW START. At the time, I didn't know anything about the philosophy. Prior to arriving there, I hadn't heard of NEW START or the 8 laws of health. I was introduced to an entirely new way of thinking that helped me create new habits and break old ones. I was also in an environment that allowed me to focus on forming better lifestyle habits that would lead to better health in the long-run. I had a wake-up call, and the reality was, if I was going to beat cancer, I needed to get my mind locked in. It wasn't going to be easy, but life was the only option.

The first day we arrived at Eden's Valley was light. It was all about getting settled in and understanding how the community functioned. I had a chance to get to know the people who would be going through the program with me. It was a great bonding experience for us all. I found out quickly how strong faith was in the community. Everything took God and belief into consideration. We had daily devotions and lectures.

On the first night, we met for a Trust and Healing meeting. We all put our names in a hat and chose a person to pray for during the entire program. We revealed who we prayed for at the end of. This set the tone for me because I knew that I had someone out there lifting me in prayer. I was also gifted with the opportunity to do the same thing for someone else. It was a great way for me to begin this new journey I was on.

1:30 Lunch at Dining Hall: 1:30 PM

When I arrived in the dining area, I was finally able to see all the people who were in our program. In the beginning, there was about 9 of us. Some of us were in the cancer treatment or wellness program, and others were support people of someone enrolled in the program. We had people from the Bahamas, Jamaica, Canada, Uganda, Haiti, and a variety of places from around the United States. I had no idea how close we would become over the next few weeks.

As we sat for our first meal, I was informed that a large portion of what we would be eating was grown right there on the property. Most of our food was as fresh as possible. Our menu was plant based and vegan diet. I had already adjusted my diet, but this was a level that I had not yet reached.

We ate a salad that day that was filled with a ton of fresh ingredients and marked the beginning of my new lifestyle. Little did I know that salad on would be my last meal until Wednesday morning. We all ate and returned to our room so we could rest. I focused on getting my mind ready for the journey ahead. I felt I was at the point of no return, and I had to go all in to reach my goal of defeating cancer.

2:27 PM

Joe asked me if I wanted to take a hike before orientation was scheduled to begin. I was all in. My neighbor in the house, Ron, who was in his late 70s, joined us.

We walked over to the hiking trail, and we started our hike to the top of Pancake Peak. It was close to a mile to the top, and when we reached, I stood and took in the view. From the top of the peak, I saw all 600 acres of property. It was beautiful and peaceful. Shortly after, we had to make our way back to the lecture hall for orientation. Everything was a strategic and we were adhering to a tight schedule.

4:00 Meet your therapist

Later that day, I found out that Joe was my personal therapist for the next 2 weeks. He would be available to assist me with the process and encourage me throughout the journey. I was relieved because Joe and I connected at the airport already, so I knew we were already on our way to cultivating a healthy rapport and relationship. We went over the expectations for the week and looked at the schedule.

6:00 Broth at LSC

6:15 Trust and Healing

6:30 DVD Lecture series LSC

7:30 Goodnights

9:00 Bedtime

After a long day of travel, I was looking forward to my bedtime on the first night. I knew that the next day was going to be a challenge that required rest and focus. I had a nice and quiet space that allowed me to rejuvenate and refresh as I got ready for the new journey.

Monday, September 6th - First full day at Eden's Valley

The first full day at Eden's Valley was a stretch compared to the relaxed approach I had in my personal life. I had to adjust my entire mindset to get up before the dawn and get active. Also, on Monday and Tuesday, we did a juice fast. Instead of daily meals, we had juice every 2 hours. Being on a tight schedule and not eating for 2 days was already trying. But I understood and knew it was impossible to embrace a NEW START with the same old habits.

My first full day was as follows:

| | |
|---|---|
| 5:45 – Wake and drink lemon water | **Wake and Drink lemon water - 5:45 am**. Waking up daily in the house at 5:45 was a struggle. I had my own room but shared a house with 4 other people. I could hear them already up and moving while I was still tucked in under the covers. I finally dragged myself out of bed and proceeded to get my day started. Each day began with designated vitamins and therapeutics. Then, we got ready to head to the Life Center by 6:20. We all had different things we had to take each day and we worked to support each other. We became a family over the 2-week period and our daily family meeting started in the kitchen at 5:45am. |
| 6:20 | **6:20 am** We left our living quarters and took the short walk to the Life Center where we connected with the other members of the program who were housed in different locations. We had morning detox tea and devotion to start our day that consisted of a spiritual dialogue. Even though I was not raised as a 7th day Adventist, I loved, admired, and respected their discipline and approach to health and wellness. There were many people in my |

program who knew the bible, scriptures, and theology. I was impressed by their knowledge and love for God. It was inspiring. It made me disciplined to deepen my connection with the Most High and become more discipled and focused.

| | |
|---|---|
| 7:00 | **Morning walk- 7:00 am** After morning devotion, we took a walk. Although our group was quite diverse, I was one of the youngest there. I often tried to push myself and compete with myself because I was half the age of most of those around me. I realized early on that I had to push myself based on my personal expectations and not anyone else's because the program was meant to be tailored for each individual. So, even if I walked ahead or at a faster pace, I always doubled back to unite with my tribe. |
| 7:30 | **Juice at dining hall-**<br><br>**7:30** am After our walk, it was time to head to the dining hall. If it was Monday and Tuesday, our breakfast consisted of juice. On the other days, we had breakfast together. Eden's Valley changed my perspective on breakfast. I grew up eating bacon, |

eggs, pancakes, waffles, cereal, and toast in the mornings. But I was exposed to a new level of thinking when it came to breakfast. We had mixed berries with nuts and seeds for starters. Then, we had beans and legumes. I felt myself becoming energized after each meal.

Breakfast also became another time to strengthen community relationships. We encouraged each other, shared wins, and made plans for the day.

| | |
|---|---|
| 8:30 | Lecture at dining hall - **8:30 am** After finishing our morning meal, it was time for our first lecture of the day. We had different guest speakers or lecturers who would lead for the day. We covered everything from the food we ate, the aroma therapy we used to the mindset around fighting our disease. Each day was packed with a wealth of information that could be used to enhance our lives. |
| 10:00 – 11:00 | Fever bath - **10:00 am** After the lecture was finished, it was time for my first appointment of the day. I started my day with the fever bath The fever was one of the first real challenges I encountered at Eden's Valley—apart from waking up unnaturally |

early. The fever bath aimed to improve circulation and help boost the immune system. Since my white blood cell count was low as a result of chemotherapy, I was looking forward to the process. I was scheduled for 9 sessions over a 2-week period of time.

In the fever bath, we sat in a tube of water between 110 and 112 degrees until we reached a fever temperature. After reaching a fever temperature, we would hold the temperature in our body for about twenty minutes before starting the cool down process. The entire process usually took about an hour to complete.

My first fever bath taught me a lot about myself. When I first stepped into the water, I questioned if I was going to be able to submerge my entire body into the hot water. I had never done anything like that before. I went down very slow and I felt the hot water touch ever part of my skin as I sank down into it until the only thing outside the water was my head.

After a few minutes, my body started to adjust. I sat there in the water and waited for my internal body temperature to rise. It felt like I was in the water for an hour. It was getting hard to breathe and I was getting irritated. When he checked my internal temperature, it was barely above normal and there was little impact. When I checked the time, only 10 minutes had passed. I knew in my mind that I wasn't going to make it. I started getting antsy in the water and moving around. Joe checked my temperature again and it was rising towards a fever. I pushed myself as far as I could go before finally giving up for the day.

I got out of fever bath feeling defeated. I realized that my body was capable of handling the heat and pressure, but I had a weak mentality. If I was going to fight and beat cancer, I had to work on my mindset. Cancer was a lot tougher than a fever bath.

Over the course of the next 2 weeks, I improved on my time in the fever bath. I realized that if I told myself before I got in the water that I was sure about making it the entire time, I would fail quick and be out of the water. On the days I set my goal to beat the previous day's record, I achieved it. The days I questioned if I could be the previous day were a mental struggle. I started to focus on pushing myself to the max and not doing what felt comfortable.

By the time I was done with the ninth fever bath, I noticed my personal growth and development. I felt accomplished because I questioned myself so much. I was doubting myself and talking myself out of success. When I reversed the conversation I was having with myself, my results changed for the better. I was able to reap the benefits of the fever bath by overcoming my self-doubt and sabotage.

| | |
|---|---|
| 11am to 1pm | Juice at residence - **11 am to 1 pm.** After spending an hour with the fever bath process, I was always tired and drained. Since I had a 2-hour break, I returned to my room and used the infrared dome for an hour as I took a nap. I laid down on the bed and placed the dome over my entire midsection. The done was said to send infrared light beneath the skin into to the body, which helped destabilize cancer cells. This gave me a chance to rest and try a therapeutic approach that could help me in my fight against cancer. Those daily nap sessions gave me a boost in my energy for the remainder of the day. |
| 1:00 pm Daily exercise and workout - | Daily exercise and workout - **1-1:30 pm.** After the break, it was time to work out for the day. I woke from my nap and walked to the gym. Every person was at a different skill level, but we all pushed each other based on each person's ability. We understood everyone was on a different path and still found a way to encourage each other through the workouts. Our focus was on high intensity interval training (HIIT). We completed a high energy and effort |

| | |
|---|---|
| | activity and then took a break. We learned things we could do at home even if we didn't have gym equipment. I was able to add some new activities to my tool belt as I worked to improve my health. |
| 1:30 | Juice in the dining hall or lunch – Each day after working out, we headed to the dining hall for either juice or a nutritious meal, depending on the day. |
| 2:30 | Hyperbaric oxygen chamber – **2:30 to 3:30 pm.** After finishing up our nutritious meal for the day, it was time for my hyperbaric oxygen therapy (HBOT) session. During the session, I climbed inside a chamber that looked like a big tube and laid down. The chamber was zipped up and I was locked inside for an hour looking at nothing but the top of the tube. I am not a fan of being locked in closed spaces. The first day, I felt like I was going to suffocate. It felt like the walls were going to close in on me. But I found a soundtrack that I liked, and I laid back and zoned out to the music. Before I knew it, it was over. |

In order for me to embrace the Hyperbaric Oxygenation chamber, I had to understand the purpose and how it was beneficial. I enjoyed the nap, but I wanted to know more. I found that HBO restored blood supply to the compromised region enabling the body to alter the course and impact of the disease process. For me, it was worth the time spent inside the tube. I had a total of 9 HBOT sessions. Not only did my body reap the benefits, but I also grew mentally by overcoming a personal issue of triggered claustrophobia when in tight spaces.

|  |  |
|---|---|
| | Juice at residence |
| 3:30 | Physician consult, massage session or business center meeting. |
| | **3:30 pm – 4:30 pm** After the HBOT session, the next activity varied depending on the day. I either had a consult with the physician, a massage session, or a meeting with a staff member. I found both to be useful for my overall health. |

During the physician consult, I had the opportunity to bring together the naturopathic perspective and mix it with the medical perspective to create a game plan for moving forward. Dr. Keith worked in both fields and helped me bring a balanced perspective to my decision-making process. Dr. Keith was the first doctor who ever prayed for me. When we met, I brought all my documentation and lab work from the CTCA so he could help me decipher what it all meant. We talked about the lifestyle changes and diet I needed to make for optimal health.

During one of my last consults with Dr. Keith, I asked him a question. I asked him what the biggest threat to my life was based on what he saw from looking at my documentation. He told me something that really stuck with me. Dr. Keith said that the longevity of my life was not based on what was currently in my body but based on what I do what I put in my body moving forward. He then referred me back to the lecture and the 8 laws of health. He encouraged me to customize a NEW START program. The knowledge, compassion, and prayers that Dr. Keith displayed were all unexpected blessings that added value to my treatment program.

If not meeting with Dr. Keith, another option for this time slot was a massage therapy session. The sessions lasted about an hour or so and the masseuse was amazing. I was able to get some aches and pains that had been bothering me for months worked out. I realized how vital it was for my body to add the massage therapy as often as possible. It was not only good for my body but also good for my mind.

During this time slot, we met with the lady I called our counselor, therapist, aunt, and mother, Mrs. Brenda. She reminded me of a family member. She was kind, loving, understanding, and stern. She had a military background that impacted her discipline and focus. She made sure that we had a plan to transition back home so we would maintain our healthy habits. Mrs. Brenda helped maintain the long-term effects of what was learned at Eden's Valley, and she still calls me to this day. She holds

| | |
|---|---|
| | me accountable, gives me advice, shows me support, and always prays over me. |
| 6:00 | Broth at Lifestyle Center – 6:00 Broth at LSC<br><br>I learned quickly that we only get 2 meals per day. One at 7:30 am and another at 1:30pm. At 6:00 each day, we met for our last meal of the day: broth. The rule was to eat breakfast like a king, lunch like a queen, and dinner like a baby. I was used to eating in a window from 11am to 8pm but I quickly adjusted to this. |
| 6:15 | Trust and Healing afternoon devotion - 6:15 Trust and Healing<br>The Trust and Healing session was a nice devotional moment where all the members of the program came together, fellowshipped, and community built. We shared, read the bible, and prayed with and for each other. It was a great way for us to stay connected. |
| | DVD Lecture series - Each night, we had lectures on health and wellness. This was the foundation and |

| | |
|---|---|
| 6:30 | introduction to a NEW START and the 8 laws of health. I had seen and heard the term all day but during the lecture series by Brenda O'Neal, I started to understand what it meant and stood for. |

(NEW) N- Nutrition E- Exercise W- Water

(START) S- Sun T- Temperance A- Air R- Rest T- Trust

Over the next 14 days, I got information that changed my entire life from these lectures alone. Given what I was learning, I had no excuses for continuing with some of my previous habits. I knew it was time for a NEW START.

Goodnight – dismiss for the day. 7:30 Goodnights

| | |
|---|---|
| 7:30 | After the lecture was over, it was time to say our goodbyes and good nights and return to our individual living quarters. This was the official end to our day of activities. This gave us time to get settled in for the day and reflect on the day's activities. |
| 9:00 | Bedtime - |

9:00 Bedtime

After a long day of activities, I was looking forward to my bedtime each day. Even though I usually had a hard time falling asleep in the new environment, each night I rested well because the days were packed with activities.

Each day during the entire program followed a similar scheduled. Some activities were exchanged for others, but the basics of the schedule remained constant. And although each day had a similar schedule, each day was its own journey. I had the opportunity to embrace each journey and build connections that will last a lifetime. I found an adopted family that continues to inspire and encourage me. It was a challenge to adjust from a lifetime of habits to forming a new mindset around life and health. Having a strong family support system is vital in achieving this. I found that family at Eden's Valley.

The time I spent away from my family at Eden's Valley gave me a chance to think and reflect. I kept a video journal to document the information I was learning about and to help me process my thoughts. Through the physical and mental journey, I was able to validate that the human mind and body are amazing. They can be used to help you reach any goals and learn how to live a more sustainable life. With the right focus, you can reach your financial, spiritual, and fitness goals. And you'll survive if you happen to encounter a life-threatening disease like cancer.

## Heading Home

After spending 2 weeks at Eden's Valley, it was time to return home and practice the new lifestyle changes I learned. I knew it was going to be a challenge outside a controlled environment and I knew it would require focus. I thought about what it would take to be the best version of myself. In the program, I had a full team of people who I could depend on to help me through. At home, I had a team of people who were depending on me to get the job done.

On the last day of the program, my wife and kids surprised me and drove 15 hours from Phoenix to Loveland. While I was glad to see them, I knew I would have a rocky start transitioning home. Instead of taking a less than 2-hour flight home, I now had to navigate my family all the way back to

Arizona. With 4 kids in a minivan, it wasn't long before the challenges ahead of me presented themselves front and center. The older kids were fighting and the younger kids crying. I had to breathe and adjust. I was going from an environment that was built for my healing into a situation that would require all my focus and attention to maintain consistency.

Before we left the state of Colorado, we drove into Denver and up to Madison, Wyoming. Since we were already so close to both cities, we decided to take advantage. It was my first time and so we created a new memory for our family before getting on the road. My goal was to make the most out of the situation and that is what we did. As we crept our way through the Colorado mountains, we had a chance to visit Aspen and Vail Colorado, 2 cities I always wanted to visit.

I was cautious the entire time because I knew when I returned home to Phoenix, I had a follow up with the Cancer Center and they would be doing labs and looking at my bloodwork. I didn't want to do anything that would negatively impact all the hard work I put in in Colorado . For the most part, I maintained my diet and walked 10,000 steps per day.

The day after our return was the big doctor's appointment. I was nervous to see what the results were because I chose to stop my chemotherapy and try something different—against the recommendation of the doctors.

I went in feeling confident because I felt the changes I made in my life were positive and impactful. I checked in and the nurse called me to the back for my bloodwork. She asked me how chemo was going and I informed her that I paused my treatment program to try natural options. The nurse told me that she was proud of me for taking my health into my hands and offered her congratulations. I started to feel even better about my decision.

After my blood was drawn, I went back to the lobby to wait for my doctor's appointment where we would discuss the results. The first person I met with was my surgeon. This was my first time ever meeting him because he replaced my previous surgeon who moved to a different location.

When he looked at the blood work, he was shocked. He saw that my CEA, a measure of a hormone that helps determine if the cancer is growing or not, was drastically lower. Mine went from 8.9 to 4.2 in a month. The normal range is 3.8 or lower. My white blood cell count that was dangerously low before doubled and I was out of the danger zone of being vulnerable to simple infections.

I informed the doctor that I paused my chemo and tried some natural options. I went on to tell him about all the different things I applied. I told him about the diet changes and the vitamins I was taking. He was impressed by the discipline and the results. He felt we needed to order a new round of scans to see if there was a change in my tumor on my colon or the lesions on my liver.

The next appoint was with my oncologist who oversaw the administration of my chemotherapy. When I paused chemo, she warned me about the possibilities of what could happen. She was also concerned we might lose the progress we had already made. They were valid concerns, and I appreciated the fact that she even cared. When she looked at the blood work, she was shocked, as well. The numbers were amazing. Every possible thing that could have improved in my favor did. She wanted to continue with the treatment program, but I opted to wait until we could see the scans.

The surgeon and oncologist got together and approved to have another round of scans done even though it was sooner than they had scheduled. I came back a few days later and completed the scans. On the first scan, 3 out of the 4 cancer spots in my body were barely visible and required an additional scan to get a closer look. It was definitive proof that the program at Eden's Valley had a major impact on my health. I decided to keep chemo paused and even postponed all surgical procedures until further notice. I decided I would take the naturopathic route as far as it would take me. It was a bold move and one not everyone was on board with.

The doctors also ordered another colonoscopy to get a closer look at the original spot the cancer was located. The tumor in my colon was smaller and was shrinking. I was feeling good about my decision to go natural, but I knew it was going to be a grind moving forward. I kept all my appointments with the Cancer Center so I could get my bloodwork and scans done as needed. I was under medical surveillance as I monitored my labs and bloodwork.

When I got the labs and bloodwork back, I followed my script of checking what was abnormally low or high. I then found solutions to help improve that area. It wasn't long before I was taking over twenty pills per day. But it was clearly working.

## My Birthday in October

For my 44th birthday, some of my friends and family flew out to Phoenix to visit me. We rented a million-dollar home in Scottsdale, Arizona and had a great time enjoying each other's company. At the property, we had amenity space including a huge backyard, pool table, swimming pool, hot tub, and even a basketball court. Since I was still immuno-compromised, we wanted to find a spot that would allow us to enjoy the space and each other's company.

My 2 younger brothers, Darious and Donald Jr came and stayed at the house for the extended weekend. My college friends, Tyson Barrett, Mendez Hollis, and Quentin Henry, all joined us. My cousin, Tristan, and my childhood friend from my hometown, Kelvin Davis, who we all refer to as Squash was also there. This celebration was special and different.

The truth of the matter was that I didn't know how many more birthdays I had before me. I embraced every second as we laughed and celebrated another year of life.

During the weekend, I got some of the therapy and love I needed along my journey. We took full advantage of the house and stayed to the very last minute before leaving and returning to the reality of life. I knew I had a doctor's appointment the day after the last guests flew out. I was careful over the weekend to make sure I stayed as disciplined as possible. I learned that you could have a good time and still handle your business of focusing on health.

After the last airport run, it was time to get back to the hardcore focus on my health. I wanted to be able to celebrate many more birthdays. I locked in and got ready for my venture back to the CTCA.

My bloodwork was stable for the most part as I struggled to maintain the strict diet and workout routine. I was able to keep a close eye on my labs every 2 weeks when I went in for checkups. With the stress of family life, I saw the good habits start to become more and more inconsistent. One day, I found myself dealing with a ton of stress. My wife and I were not on the same page and the stress of having 4 kids was starting to affect me. When I went for a checkup, I noticed some of my numbers and bloodwork were starting to rise. At this point, I knew I had to make some decisions.

I continued to evaluate my current lifestyle and habits. I knew that the stress of my household and marriage was not good for my healing. I knew I was risking my life if I continued the same trend. I took some time to evaluate all my options and came up with a game plan. I was facing stage 4 cancer in my body and stage 4 cancer in my marriage at the same time. I started to feel vulnerable. It was as if I was losing the battle and I knew it was time to take a bold action.

After looking into all my options, I knew I had to decide based on what was the best path for me. I knew that the medical doctors were going to push one thing and my naturopathic team were going to push another. And so, I decided to make my own decision and create a plan that worked best for me. I took a few days alone to think about my decision before I told anyone what it was. I learned that a lot of people's support was linked to the path they wanted for me, not the path I wanted for myself. I decided to wait at least 24 hours before disclosing my decision so I could prepare myself for the pushback I would inevitably receive.

I decided to contact the surgeon and tell him I was ready to move forward with the procedure. I was contacted by someone from his tea, and within days, I was put on the surgical calendar. I was not mentally prepared for the process, and I was feeling uncomfortable with my journey.

The doctor called to discuss the procedure and we set up an appointment to meet at the Cancer Center. Even though we were not exactly on the same page about my treatment program, my wife accompanied me to the doctor's appointment. As I sat in the meeting with the doctor, he started to explain what I would be going through. He gave me the best case scenario and the worst case scenario. I was in disbelief as I listened to his detailed explanation of the things that would happen to me during the procedure. As he continued on, I started feeling sick. I passed out as he lifted my shirt to show me where he was going to cut.

When I awoke, I was confused about what had happened. I thought I was on stage delivering a speech and forgot what I was talking about. I had to take a few minutes to gather my thoughts and then it dawned on me. I passed out…again.

I was getting ready to face 2 of my biggest fears. I was going to have an invasive surgery and had to deal with the extreme pain that came along with it. The doctor explained that he would remove the lesions out of my liver first. Then, he would move into my colon where he would remove a section and then reconnect my digestive system. I was very uncomfortable, but I had made my decision. I was going through with the process.

The next few weeks were spent on mentally and physically preparing for the surgery and the recovery process I was to face. The first thing I committed to was reaching a weight of

205 pounds before the surgery. I had been weighing in at a number below 200 pounds and knew I needed to get the numbers on the scale back up to speed up my recovery afterward. I was looking at about a 2-week period until my surgery to achieve all that I wanted to in preparation for the procedure.

The week prior to my surgery, I set a goal to walk 100,000 steps in the 7 days leading up to the procedure. I found different areas to walk around. I drove to downtown Phoenix and walked for miles. I went to Tempe and walked the boardwalk on the lake and the main street. I went to Scottsdale, Arizona and walked around the mall. I walked in all major stores and took a tour as I collected my steps. I blew my step goal out of the water. In 2 days, I had already walked almost 60,000 steps and reached 100,000 within 5 days.

As the days quickly ticked off the calendar, I mentally prepared myself by praying and staying relaxed. Walking each day was a huge help as I was able to focus my mind on getting ready for a new experience. I made arrangements to stay at my father's house to recover and I moved in with him and my stepmother prior to the surgery. My wife and I were still not doing well and I needed a place I could focus on healing and recovering. I was about to go through the most stressful experience of my life and needed peace to maximize my healing. Finding that space with marital issues and 4 small kids was difficult. I had to decide to save my life first and focus on saving my marriage after.

Staying at my father's house was great at first. I was able to get my rest and get my mind focused on what was to come. There was little conflicting energy as I counted down the days to the surgery. I had my own room and space at the back of the house. I tried to stay out of the way as much as possible leading up to the surgery. I always hated the feeling of being a burden and didn't want to wear out my welcome.

## Surgery Time

I met with a friend and colleague, Jasaund Emanuel, for lunch at the Biltmore area in Phoenix the day before my surgery. I didn't know if that was going to be my last meal or not. But I had faith that I would make it out. I was conscious of both sides of the coin during that meal. I knew that the reality was I could live or I could die.

After we ate, I headed back to my resting spot. It was time to prepare for the procedure, which was 24 hours away. I packed my bag and made sure I had everything I needed for a stay at the hospital. I was scheduled to be there for under a week. I was not in a rush to leave and wanted to stay as long as I needed to ensure I was ready to go home.

I had to drink a horrible mixture beforehand to clean my insides out. It was supposed to be flavored, but it had a horrible aftertaste. I struggled to get the first dose down. Then, a few hours later, I had to repeat the process and take another dose. I struggled to consume all the liquid and felt sick after I drank it all. It definitely cleaned me out as I was in and out of the restroom for hours. I lost 3 pounds from the time I started until my body was empty.

On the day of the surgery, my father took me to the CTCA for my procedure. My day started with a Covid-19 test at 5:30 am. After the results came back negative, I was taken in with a nurse and led to the room where I would be prepped and briefed. I was nervous but I had to focus on healing and becoming cancer free. The nurses were all very nice and compassionate. They made sure I was comfortable and answered all my questions to make sure I was relaxed and in the best mindset for the procedure. All the doctors came in to explain their role and make sure I was still on board with the process.

I had some necessary and uncomfortable conversations to ensure that things would go as planned if I didn't make it out. I had to think about my kids and securing their futures. I had to operate and stand in pure faith as I got ready to go under.

The time arrived. My surgeon came in and gave me the last update. A nurse then came over and put something into my IV. I felt myself getting a bit woozy.

They rolled me back into the operating room. I had no recollection of anything that happened during the 10 hours I was under. The doctor took his time to go through my liver and look for all the cancer he could find. They located the 3 areas of cancer that were picked up on the scan and removed them. About 15 to 20% of my liver was removed.

After he was done, they moved to my colon. The process required my colon to first be cut in half and the section where the cancer was located was removed. After the impacted segment was removed, the colon would then be stitched back together. I was then glued and stitched up.

## Waking Up From Surgery

I woke up from the surgery after being out of the world for almost half a day. When I opened my eyes, I was confused about what was going on. I vaguely remember seeing my father in the room talking with the doctor. They confirmed it went well but I was in no position to understand what that meant. I was in and out of consciousness as the medicine wore off. My neck and the back of my head were sore from laying down in the same position for so long.

I was rolled into the room I'd be staying in over the next few days to recover. I was given 3 milestones to meet before I could go home. I had to pass gas, have a bowel movement, and be able to walk on my own. I still couldn't eat, so my diet was primarily liquid and much of my hydration was given via the IV. After I was settled in, the doctor came by and checked on me. He let me know he needed me to get up and walk. I had just awoke from a ten-hour procedure and now I had to walk. I was mentally unprepared, but I knew I had to do it. My legs needed circulation and so did the rest of my body. It was a real struggle to stand and get out of bed. I was moving slower than ever. My stomach was really sore, and the meds had not yet completely wore off. As I stood, I felt off balance and a dizzy. I had to use a walker to stand and walk. I was taking very small steps and I worked with my physical therapist to walk to the door. When I finally made it to the door, my therapist set a goal for me to walk about 50 steps and back to the bed for the day. As I did so, there was another gentleman who was also walking around the floor. He made 2 laps around the entire floor before I could get about halfway through my goal. I looked at him and how fast he was walking, and I thought, *I can't wait to be able to walk like that.* At first, I was comparing myself to him and his progress. What I later found out was that he had been there for a few days already and was further along in his recovery. I could not compare myself to him because we both had different procedures, on different day, and different body types.

After the short walk, I stumbled back to the bed and laid down. I passed out for the night because I was still tired, and I had a variety of medicines being pumped into my body. The nurses came in and checked on me frequently. I slept in small spurts between the check ins and medicine administration but found myself struggling to get into a deep sleep. I struggled, tossing and turning all night.

The next day started with another walk. I was able to walk much further and faster and was mentally determined to recover. I started to push myself because I realized that my desire to and ability to get up were impacted by my thoughts. I changed my thought process and went for it. I felt my body bouncing back and getting stronger already. I was still using the walker and could not walk alone but I was making progress.

On the second day of recovery, I was able to stand and walk without the walker. I met one of my milestones. Then, my bowels woke up and I started to pass gas. I felt my body going through the changes by the day. I was more in tune to my body and what was going on. I still had the catheter in, but it had to be removed since I was able to get up and walk around. This was a very uncomfortable experience. First, it was my first time having a tube inside my penis and now I had to watch it be removed. As the nurse came around and got into position, I instinctively shut my eyes. I felt a pulling sensation and thought it was over. But I didn't realize she was just getting started. I was shocked at how far it was inside my body. Before I could gasp or react, it was pulled all the way out. I felt a slight burning and an urge to urinate.

The first time I used the bathroom on my own, I felt and heard the air pockets inside of my penis as I forced the urine out. I had to get used to using the restroom on my own because for the last 3 days, I was going in a tube without even realizing I was being emptied.

By the third day, I managed to eat a low fiber diet. I still wasn't feeling hungry, but I realized I needed to eat. I started out with peaches and water. I wasn't able to eat salad or certain fruits for a few days. My first official meal was baked salmon and mashed potatoes. I didn't eat very much of it, but I was glad that I was able to finally eat something without feeling incredibly sick. The medicine I was on had my body confused and my stomach feeling off.

During my recovery, I also experienced hot and cold flashes. I went from sweating right into a cold freeze where I was shivering. A few minutes later, I became hot again. This had me feeling very uncomfortable and contributed to my lack of sleep.

But when I did fall asleep, I had some of the most random and crazy dreams. I went to places and met people who I had never met before. One night, I dreamed I was in New York City with Busta Rhymes and we picked up Nikki Minaj in Rolls Royce. It seemed so real. I woke up and realized that I was not only in the hospital bed but in pain and had to use the restroom. The dreams kept coming and I had to find a strategy to help control my thoughts. I turned to music. I found and created soundtracks that mellowed me out and allowed my mind and body to relax. This helped me relax and get better rest each night.

On Saturday, December 4th, I was excited because of the SEC championship game featuring Georgia Bulldogs and

Alabama. It gave me something to look forward to. My brother was also coming by to watch the game with me. There were several games on that day, so, I decided to get up early and try to move around and get my exercise in so I could spend some time watching.

As I sat in the chair watching one of the first games of the day, I felt a sensation in my stomach that felt like I had to pass gas, which was a good thing. This time, it was much more. In a matter of seconds, I reached my third milestones as I used the bathroom all over myself. I had already been warned about the possibility and it had quickly turned into a reality. My stomach was will ready to be emptied as I struggled to get out of the chair and into the bathroom. There was a call button in the bathroom, and I needed help. I called the nurse on duty, and he came in right away and found the mess.

There was a mess on the floor, the chair, and the covers I was using. I stood there with a black tar-like substance filling my underwear and running down my legs. He didn't even pause. He jumped right in, helped me get on the toilet, and while I sat there to empty myself, he went in to clean my room.

This was the first time I sat on the toilet after the procedure. Every time I pushed, it hurt from the inside. As I sat there, pushing in pain, I was humbled by the experience. I was in a position where I used the bathroom on myself and couldn't wipe my own butt. This was the day after I watched a stranger pull a tube out of my penis.

Two nurses from the shift got my room cleaned up and the other nurse came in and helped me get cleaned up. He had to wipe my butt down and help me take a shower. I was still connected to the IV and bandaged up so I was limited in what I could do. My nurse was amazing. He cleaned me up, helped me get dressed, got me back up in my bed, and called to have my room sanitized. Even though it wasn't how I envisioned it, I reached my third milestone, and I was one step closer to going home.

Later that day, my brother, Donald, came by, and we watched the Georgia game. My brother who worked in the rehabilitation and medical field for years was the perfect person to help me get up and moving. That day, I walked more than the previous day. We set a goal and went with it. I walked almost 1000 steps that day, which made me realize that I had more mental control over the process. I started to leverage my mindset to help push me out of the comfort associated with lying down. My body responded in a positive way. The challenge was to harness the power of my mind. It was a process, and I realized my strong mind could become a liability if I pushed too much. Balance was the key to success.

After a long day of activity, I was looking forward to sleeping that night. I tried to stay up and not nap as much during the day so I could get better rest during the night. I was waking up every 10 to twenty minutes for hours at a time. I wanted to sleep for a good 4 hours straight. But I was scheduled to take medicine every 6 hours and most of the time, I had to have my vitals taken, as well. This all required me to be awake. I asked the nurse for something to help me sleep. She gave me what we thought was a low dose of Benadryl. My body started to respond with the hot and cold flashes, and I got sick. I threw up and felt nauseous for a while before finally passing out.

The next day, my brother stopped by to drop off a few items just as the doctor was coming by for a visit. It was at that moment that they realized my extreme sensitivity to the medicine I was taking. I decided to stop taking all the medicine except for a scheduled muscle relaxer and Tylenol. I knew I would be going home soon so I wanted to manage the pain before leaving. I didn't want to take unnecessary pills, so, I cut out as many as possible. I was officially unhooked from the IV and all liquid pain medicines. I had a tube in the side of my stomach that ran inside my body. I tried not to look at it, but it was connected to a tube that ran into a drainage container. It collected blood and other fluids that were inside my body. The doctor was now ready to remove the tube from my side.

As he walked around and prepared to remove it, again, I found my eyes instinctively closing. I turned my head to the side as he examined the area. I felt him touching the area and then I felt the tube sliding out of the side of my stomach area. It didn't hurt but I certainly felt it. I was happy I didn't pass out. He put a Band-Aid over the spot and said it would close on its own in a few days. Just like that, I was tube free. I could get up and walk without a walker and I had no tubes hanging from or connected to my body.

The night before I prepared to leave, I was off all medications except for Tylenol and the muscle relaxers. I had the best night's sleep since my procedure. I was able to sleep for hours at a time and didn't take any pain medicine. The crazy dreams and the cold and hot flashes from the previous nights were gone. I was ready to go home.

The next day, I was cleared for release and my father and stepmom came by to pick me up. I was bandaged and packed, ready to leave as soon as possible. At that point, I hadn't been outside in nearly 6 days. I was able to walk all the way from my hospital room to the car. My first stop after leaving the Cancer Center was to get my favorite strawberry and banana smoothie from Bosa's Donuts.

I had planned to stay at my father's house for the first couple weeks before returning home to my wife and kids. When we got back to the house, I went into my room in the back. My room was ready to go, and my mission was to find a comfortable position to sleep. At the hospital, I could adjust my bed and find a comfortable spot. At home, I didn't have that same luxury and needed to find a way to get some rest. My father had a recliner in the room next to where I was sleeping so I rotated from the bed to the recliner.

Each day I spent at my father's house allowed me to get stronger. By the end of the first week, I could walk up to 8,000 steps. I was off the pain pills and was able to maintain a light diet. After the first week of recovery, I felt the vibe and knew it was time to go home before I wore out my welcome. My son, Noah, came over and stayed the last night with me and the next day, we packed up and went home.

My son told me he was tired of being the man of the house and wanted me home. I felt bad for leaving my wife alone with the kids, but I felt it would have been worse if I had passed away and left them permanently. I had to be selfish for a while to ensure I was healthy enough to be an asset to my household.

I returned home to my wife and kids and a house full of activity. I wasn't yet fully recovered but I did my part to help as much as possible. I bought a recliner chair to sit and sleep in because laying in the bed wasn't comfortable. It felt good to be home, but it was much different from my previous environments. I had to adjust to being back as a part of my household.

I took it as slow as possible to allow my body to heal. After being home with my wife and kids for 3 days, it was time for my follow up at the Cancer Center. I met with my surgeon, and he looked at my bloodwork from my labs and surveyed my surgical wounds. He said the surgery went well and he was pleased with the results. I was scheduled to come back in 2 weeks for another follow up.

The time between doctors' appointments was spent walking and getting my body back to a healthy strength. I set a goal to walk 10,000 steps per day for 100 days as part of my physical and mental rehab. I had a chance to spend time with my kids and reconnect with my family. My daughter, Eden, and oldest son, Noah, were a huge help with the younger kids. I know the process was rough on them and I appreciate their assistance through the journey.

Over the next week, I realized that I was starting to snack and eat more than usual. I found myself slipping and realized I wasn't maintaining the same discipline as before. For New Year's, we decided to take a family trip to California. While they indulged in bad eating habits, Noah said, "Dad, you haven't been eating healthy lately." He was right. I wasn't eating as healthy as I should have been to maintain and progress towards optimal health. For the remainder of the trip, I was more conscious of what I was putting into my body and tried to think and apply the laws of health to my recovery.

Two days after returning home from California, I was scheduled for another follow up with my surgeon who performed my procedure and the oncologist who administered my chemotherapy. I usually had someone with me when I went because of the times I passed out, but this day, I went alone. I prayed in the parking lot and went inside. I checked in like always, then, I went to the lab to have my blood drawn. I went back out to the lobby and waited to see the first doctor after my lab results came back.

About an hour later, it was time to meet with my surgeon. He told me that he was pleased with my progress and the results from my bloodwork. My CEA levels were at 2, which was well within the range. I had never seen it that low before.

At that moment, I was ready to ask the doctor the question I had been waiting to ask since I was diagnosed. I knew doctors were hesitant about using the phrase *cancer free*, so I asked him if there was any measurable cancer inside my body. He said, "No, we see no detectable cancer in your body, which is consistent with the bloodwork we see from your labs." I had been praying for those words. I could not have asked for a better result, outcome, or feedback from the doctor. I thanked God for blessing me and the doctor for his part in saving my life. I didn't even have the urge to celebrate the victory because I knew the journey was just beginning. I had to work to maintain a lifestyle that would allow me to keep the cancer undetectable.

After meeting with my surgeon, I met with my oncology team about my decision for chemo. My team genuinely cared about me and my wellbeing, so, I took what they said into careful consideration. They gave me their medical feedback about the direction they felt I should go. The team felt that chemo could clean up anything that the surgery left behind and help decrease the chances of it coming back. After considering all my options, I decided to pause the chemo and go under surveillance. I would continue to get my labs, bloodwork, and scans done at the Cancer Center, but I decided I would not be taking any more chemo at that time.

Even though there was no detectable cancer in my body, and I was not going to be on chemo for the time being, I still realized I had a lot of work to do. I could not just sit back and say the battle was over because I could easily slip back into my old habits and be 240 pounds again before I knew it. I knew I needed a plan and a long-term strategy to stay healthy and cancer free. It was time to embrace a NEW START.

As my mindset shifted into a NEW START, I found myself struggling to maintain it. I realized that having the mindset was not enough; I needed a strategy. I took out my notes from Eden's Valley, reviewed the video lectures, and started to create a plan to help me reach my lifestyle goals.

# STAGE 4

# *The N.E.W. S.T.A.R.T. Process*

**Embracing**
**The Eight Laws of Health**

B eating cancer was not the end of my journey. It was truly the beginning. It was a NEW START.

When it comes to keeping track of your health, it's not always easy to see exactly where you're at. Fortunately, I was introduced to Eden's Valley and the NEW START philosophy. I realized, there are plenty of different tools out there for tracking different facets of your health, but unless you know the right questions to ask, you might never find out what's really going on with your body. I can speak from experience. Not asking the right questions about my health led me to a cancer diagnosis. After years of neglect, my treatment program at Eden Valley helped me value owning my health and healing. It's impossible to think about living a healthier life and not ask yourself the right health centered questions.

The NEW START philosophy gave me a strategy to find the right questions to ask and a specific formula to follow. These questions included: What and when am I eating? How much am I sleeping? How much water am I drinking? How much daily stress am I under? What medications and vitamins am I taking? What is my mindset and thought process? Sometimes, we neglect talking about our health because we don't want to face the reality of the answer. The foundation to better health for us all starts with one question we must ask ourselves daily: "What am I going to do today to reach my health goals?"

Although I am not a doctor, I learned to apply the knowledge and information I consume. I found that mapping out a plan that includes God's laws of health, along with the principles of biology and evolution, offered a true picture of the way we should be living our lives to remain healthy and prosperous. Even though our bodies are unique, we can harness similar health habits to improve our lives, adapt to our changing environments, and remain resilient against disease.

As I went through Eden's Valley program for 2 weeks, I gained and applied information that later became part of my new lifestyle. Every day, think about the NEW START check list:

| **Nutrition** | What healthy resources did you consume today? |
|---|---|
| **Exercise** | How many steps did you get in today? Goal: 10,000/day |
| **Water** | How much water and liquid did you drink? Goal: 96 oz/day |
| **Sunshine** | How much sun did you get? Did you take supplements to help with deficiencies? Goal: 15-minute minimum |
| **Temperance** | How are you keeping your thoughts under control? What is your mindset plan for the day? |
| **Air** | Did you go outside and breathe, pray, and meditate? |
| **Rest** | How much rest did you get? Do you feel well rested? |
| **Trust** | Did you pray to reinforce your faith in the Most High? How did you reinforce trust in yourself? |

The more we learn about how things work, the more we can do those things to make ourselves healthier and more efficient. But as we make the move to a wealthier lifestyle, there are a few things we should continue to consider as we move toward a healthy, sustainable, and cost-efficient life. I take the 8 laws, what I learned, and how they have benefited me and sum them up in the following chapters. My goal is to create a blueprint for those who may be seeking other options and forms of recovery and healing like I was.

Although I implemented the NEW START philosophy into my lifestyle, I still kept my relationship with my medical professional at the Cancer Center and my primary doctor. The goal for me was to use every resource available to improve my health. While I do believe that the NEW START program can help your body heal from certain illnesses and diseases, it is not meant to replace the advice of medical professionals. I credit a combination from what I learned from the medical community and the naturopathic community for helping create a strategy to save my life in my fight against cancer.

Do your own research and customize a system that works for you. Find the right questions to ask yourself so you can self-check your health. Don't neglect the warning signs and apply the 8 laws of health. Our health is our wealth. The next 8 chapters are personal experiences based on the application of each of the laws of health. After taking months to apply the philosophy to my life, my goal was to share my resources with others the same way my team of professionals have shared their knowledge with me.

The foundation and success are based in your habits. Use the tracker to keep us with your consistency. Create daily routines and track how many days per week you execute. Get a morning, evening, meditation, and exercise routine. Write it down and track your habbits.

## HABIT TRACKER

**MORNING ROUTINE**

S  M  T  W  T  F  S

**EVENING ROUTINE**

S  M  T  W  T  F  S

**MEDITATION**

S  M  T  W  T  F  S

**EXERCISE**

S  M  T  W  T  F  S

YdrateNelson.com

# Nutrition

Although Eden's Valley focused on a more naturopathic approach to healing , they still had medical staff who contributed to a balanced perspective. I met with the doctor available twice per week while I was in the treatment program. During our first conversation, he asked me to tell him about my diet. I told him about the salad and plant-based diet I had adopted and about how I was nearly 80% vegan while also cutting out most sources of sugar from my daily life.

He looked rather confused. "Those are some pretty healthy habits, but something doesn't add up." Then, he asked, "How long have you been eating like this?"

"About 3 months," I answered.

He then looked at me with more clarity and asked me to describe my eating habits over the last 3 years, instead. So, I reflected on to my eating habits and all the things I had put in my body. I thought about all the good food I ate over the years and smiled from enjoyment.

I let him know about how much I loved hamburgers and fries. I ate them a few times per week. I loved fried chicken and soul food. I loved snacks, cookies, ice cream, and of course, pizza. As I continued to talk about my food obsession, the doctor was busy taking notes of the terrible eating habits over the course of the last 2 decades of my life.

The day I found out I had cancer, I weighed 240 pounds. I was 65 pounds overweight. My weight was a direct reflection of my eating habits. On top of being overweight, I was also pre-diabetic and dealing with a variety of vitamin and nutrient deficiencies.

I was not using food as fuel, energy, or nutrition. I was abusing food for my personal pleasure with no consideration for what it was doing to my body and my future. Nutrition was something that I considered a few times per week, at most. Eating health was not my goal. Getting full and enjoying the food was. This mindset led to bad habits that impacted my health in the long-run.

As I reflected on my diet and the terrible habits I had formed over the years, the doctor asked, "Do you think that your previous habits could have contributed to your current situation of being diagnosed with stage 4 cancer?"

Even though I knew the answer right away, I paused before responding. I was blaming myself. It was my own bad habits that led me to that point. I nodded my head in shame. Seeing the disappointment on my face, he said, "If you truly believe that you have played a role in your diagnosis, then you should also truly believe that you're capable of healing your body. You just have to be willing to do the work."

I felt empowered. After looking at all the available information and consulting with me, the doctor seemed optimistic about my ability to fight back against cancer using nutrition as my weapon.

Having fresh and healthy meals prepared daily at Eden's Valley gave me hope and a plan to begin eating more nutritious meals. I had to adopt a nutrition plan that consisted of consuming foods that would help my growth, development, and overall health. My poor nutrition was responsible for my lack of energy, digestive problems, food allergies, cancer, pre-diabetes, weight gain, and even anxiety and depression. It was time to either continue with those habits or adopt a real plan.

Our bodies metabolize nutrients to give us energy and build tissue. Healthier lifestyles are achieved when we consume a balanced, nutritious diet to maintain strength, vigor, and overall wellbeing. A lack of nutrition is related to obesity, malnutrition, and other bodily nutritional deficiencies. Following a smart diet plan, we can cope with an ongoing illness and prevent our bodies from disease.

**Embracing Good Nutrition**

Good nutrition comes from eating a variety of foods. This includes water, fats, proteins, carbohydrates, antioxidants, starches, fibers, vitamins, and minerals. These are the nutrients that provide energy to our bodies. With good nutrition, we obtain the right amount of nutrients from healthy foods in the right concentration. For adults over the age of 40, vitamin D and minerals such as calcium and iron are of vital importance. A healthy diet for most adults includes fruits and vegetables, whole grains, low-fat dairy products, lean meats, seafood, eggs, and unsalted seeds. Furthermore, good nutrition also involves avoiding processed foods like meat, full-fat dairy products, refined grains, refined sugar, and alcohol.

The foods and drinks we consume daily make up our diet. A balanced diet is crucial for preventing any nutritional deficiencies. Nutritional deficiencies can also be caused by certain health conditions, environmental contexts, or medications. Various nutritional deficiencies, such as iron deficiency anemia, vitamin C, vitamin B12, and folate, affect our blood cells. Calcium and vitamin D deficiencies affect our bones. We can get vitamin D by going out in the sun, whereas green leafy vegetables, soya drinks, and fortified flour are the sources of calcium. In my case, I had to take additional vitamin D supplements to get back on track. Those daily doses became part of my diet as I worked to improve my deficiencies.

Additionally, nutritional deficiencies can often be caused by eating foods that don't contain essential nutrients, or using drugs that interfere with the proper functioning of our bodies.

I was guilty of that for years. I loved comfort food and the feeling of being full. But most of the food I was consuming had little or no nutritional value. The processed food and sugar contradicted the nutrition my body needed.

Overconsumption of alcohol can also impact our health. When I was in my 20s, drinking large quantities of liquor and beer was the norm. We spent years doing irreversible damage to our bodies by making alcohol a part of our weekly diet. We normalized the overindulgence of alcohol to enhance our experience without the consciousness of what it was doing to our body. Over the long haul, I am pretty sure the bad diet contributed to my downward health spiral.

Many of us don't realize how unhealthy our diets can be, which can have a negative effect on our emotional wellbeing, productivity at work, and can even result in liver disease. Our bodies are a sum of all the things we consume physically and mentally. When we are eating junk food, processed food, and lots of sugar, our bodies are not getting the fuel needed to maintain good health and heal. We are hurting ourselves with our own dietary choices.

Those who maintain a healthy diet have a lower risk of obesity, heart disease, diabetes, and cancer. To prevent high blood pressure, high cholesterol levels, and the risk of heart disease and stroke, we need to significantly reduce our sodium and sugar intake. Some steps to reduce sodium and sugar include eliminating processed foods, increasing our water intake, and increasing our potassium intake. If we increase the number of fruits and vegetables and other foods in our diet, the sodium and processed sugars can be reduced. Some fruits and vegetables, such as bananas, broccoli, kale, red cabbage, and cauliflower are healthy alternatives and are high in potassium.

I personally had to accept the fact that the foods we eat play a crucial role in the development of chronic diseases. Therefore, I needed to modify my eating habits. However, I will admit that it's not easy to change our eating habits, especially if they've been engrained in our upbringing.

To ensure that I quickly reached desired results and saw an improvement in my health, I set small, realistic goals. I knew that some things in my diet had to be eliminated but changing everything at once was going to be a challenge. I had to start small and work my way up. For example, I wanted to lose forty pounds in 4 months. I created a plan that involved a reasonable weight loss target per week. I increased the number of steps I took each day, exercised, and decreased my unhealthy food intake. Over the course of about 3 and a half months, I went from over 240 pounds to somewhere below 200 pounds for the first time in twenty years. It was a gradual process that took patience, time, and effort. And so, at the beginning of 2021, I was told I was prediabetic. Then, by the end of 2021, that status reversed and my bloodwork showed no signs of a diabetes. That was all a result of the change in my mental and physical diet.

Using a combination of behaviors, such as taking the stairs or eating a salad instead of a hamburger helped me reach my goal. It's okay to feel frustrated about these diet changes in the first few weeks as your body adjusts, but you must ensure that your health goals remain at the forefront of your mind. Reward yourself with a special dinner or new fitness clothes if you lose weight. I had to give away over half of my clothes because after I reached my weight loss goal, they didn't fit anymore.

**Nutrition Takeaways**

The only way you are going to stay on top of your nutrition changes and nutritional goals is to develop a game plan. To ensure you're eating a healthy diet, record what you consume every day. Map out your meals, what you drink, and the snacks you consume as part of your weekly strategy. If necessary, consult with a dietitian or a health coach to help you follow a special diet suited towards your unique health needs. You should also consider getting an accountability partner or someone who is willing to support you and your new mission. Having that extra support could be the difference between short-term or long-term success.

Get an annual physical, checkup, and series of bloodwork done to see what deficiencies you have in your body. You are on the right track if you are getting enough calcium, eating fruits and vegetables daily, and eating whole grain and high-fiber foods. Ideally, adopting a plant-based, vegan diet would be the best approach to maximizing a nutritious strategy, but that might be hard for some to adjust to. Some simple adjustments can still add great value. Cut back on unhealthy fat and eat fish at least once a week instead of red meat, as it is rich in omega-3 fatty acids. Fish is one of the best sources of omega-3 fatty acids and when coupled with the other marine foods, it can contribute to overall heart health. It's also important that you stay active to prevent weight gain; balanced nutrition coupled with regular exercise will help you maintain optimum weight.

When I started to get back non-favorable blood work, I had to do some research on different aspects of health to find out what certain things meant. It's important to conduct your own health and nutrition research. I had to learn to avoid consuming extra fat as it could raise cholesterol, putting me at risk of life-threatening diseases. Consuming excess fat, particularly saturated fat, increases LDL (bad) cholesterol— the harmful LDL cholesterol that is linked to heart disease. Excess weight and obesity increase the risk of high LDL cholesterol. Excess fat also has negative effects on other cells, such as reducing HDL cholesterol (good) and increasing triglycerides (fat). It also causes inflammation, which could be related to the development of diseases, such as type 2 diabetes and cancer. This hits close to home for me because I was dealing with both a pre-diabetic status and a cancer diagnosis. It was obvious that I had to change to not only stop the damage done but prevent other damage from occurring.

Dark chicken, poultry skin, fatty cuts of pork, beef, lamb, milk, cheese, butter, white bread, sour cream, and baked potatoes contain extra fat. When I first got my cancer diagnosis, I cut all of them out and went vegan for a few months. I saw a definitive difference in my body and energy level. My bloodwork changed and started heading in a more positive direction. So, I encourage you to find as many healthy alternatives as possible. It's an adventure and the destination is a healthier life. Making nutrition a daily priority will be an investment that keeps paying off.

**Nutritional Game Plan – Track your intake**

1. What does your average daily diet look like? What foods do you eat every day?

2. How much water do you consume? Do you have a hydration plan?

3. Do you have any known deficiencies?

4. What vitamins do you take daily?

- Eat an abundance of fruits, vegetables, beans, and grains prepared as naturally and simply as possible.

- A variety of meals should be eaten strategically throughout the day.

- Meals should be scheduled, consistent, and timely. Meals should be about 5 hours apart to give the digestive system a chance to complete the process.

- Cut out all snacks between meals except for water.

- Cut or significantly reduce animal products including meat, dairy, eggs, butter, cheese, and other fermented dairy.

- Avoid excessive refined foods like fats, oils, white flour, salt, and excessive sugar like honey, corn syrup, and other concentrated sugars.

| | |
|---|---|
| Adopt a plant-based diet 80% of the time or more. | |
| Find an accountability partner. | |
| Create a menu and list of foods to eat. | |

Nutrition Game Plan

**Meal Ideas**. Make a list of all the nutritious foods or meals you can think of.

| Breakfast | Lunch |
|---|---|
| Dinner | Snacks |
| Drinks | Other |

Creating a meal plan for each week will help you stay consistent. If you take the time to map out a plan, you are more likely to succeed and not get drawn into mindless eating.

Weekly Meal Plan

# WEEKLY
# MEAL PLAN

| | BREAKFAST | LUNCH | DINNER |
|---|---|---|---|
| **S** | | | |
| **M** | | | |
| **T** | | | |
| **W** | | | |
| **T** | | | |
| **F** | | | |
| **S** | | | |

# Exercise

For years, I was lazy, overworked, and neglected a consistent exercise plan.

I walked around overweight and out of shape. I wasn't meeting a minimum daily step goal nor was I going to the gym. The only walking I did was normal day-to-day walking but it was never intentional. When I gained weight, I didn't get a huge stomach. My whole body simply became thicker, and I carried a lot of weight well. It didn't look like I was as overweight as I really was. I was able to hide my obesity by wearing certain types of clothes. I normalized feeling sluggish with low energy. It was just a matter of time before my bad habits caught up with me.

I had to face the facts. When you don't make exercise part of your lifestyle, you are creating a physical and mental liability. Regular exercise is beneficial for both physical and mental health. It is one of the most important things we can do to maintain our overall health in the long-run. You can choose different ways to exercise to see the most health benefits. You can include aerobic exercise in your daily routine. Staying active and fit can help improve your mood and boost your brain power. My personal goal is to average 10,000 steps per day. You need to set a small personal fitness goal and get consistent. Afterward, elevate and push yourself to the next level.

Mental health is just as important as physical health—if not more. Exercise is a good way to reduce stress and anxiety and improve your quality of sleep. Exercise has also been shown to reduce symptoms of depression and anxiety. The days when my mind is out of focus and I don't work out, my body suffers. Our mental and physical health are intertwined in our quest for wealth and prosperity.

If you haven't already figured, my favorite exercise activity is walking. Walking is one of the best ways to start working out. It is a low risk and low impact activity. You can walk any distance and at a moderate pace. Walking is free, easy, and relaxing. Try finding a park, community garden, or any large open space near your home. Get started by walking up and down the sidewalk for thirty minutes. Begin by taking short walks around your house or neighborhood. After a few days, try to increase your number of steps or the length of time you walk for. The key is to take it one step at a time and stay consistent.

Walking also will help you get some fresh air. Spending time with nature can make you feel more positive. When you are outside, you can feel the sun, the wind, and the bugs on your skin. You can smell the flowers, grass, and earth. You can even hear the birds chirping. All these things help improve your mood. Staying active keeps you in a positive mood, even after you are done with your workout.

To stay consistent and quickly achieve positive results, make a plan and split your activity up into short intervals. Various researchers recommend at least thirty minutes of moderate exercise every day or 75 minutes of vigorous exercise every week. Also, it's best to do strength training twice a week to build muscle, maintain healthy weight, and boost your metabolism.

Exercise has a variety of benefits beyond the obvious weight maintenance goal most people set. Here are some of the benefits of regular exercise for physical and mental health:

## Crucial in preventing and treating cancer

I found out early in my cancer journey that a lack of exercise was enabling my cancer growth. My body was becoming a perfect home for cancer to grow and thrive. Sitting too much increases the risk for obesity, and research shows that there is a clear link between obesity and several types of cancer. Exercise regulates hormones. Your cancer risk increases with increased levels of hormones.

One of my first attack points against cancer was to increase the amount of exercise I was engaging in. The exercise also helped me process the stress of being a stage 4 cancer fighter. The increased blood flow and weight loss helped me just as much mentally as it did physically. Working out is a key component in my desire to become and remain cancer free.

**It improves your immune system**

When I started my chemotherapy treatment program, my white blood cell count was reduced by 60%. I was very vulnerable to getting sick from simple infections. I was searching for ways to help build and boost my WBC. I found studies showing that regular exercise could help fight infections. Running helps increase the amount of antibodies your body produces and carries to the site of an infection. Exercising also increases the number of good gut bacteria in your body, which has an indirect effect on your immune system. To reap the benefits, try getting up to a half-hour of exercise every day. It's also important that you don't overdo it or else you will be at risk of overtraining, which causes your body to withdraw the energy needed for fighting infections while also suppressing your immune system. By committing to consistent forms of exercise, I was able to get my WBC back up and maintain it moving forward. I noticed that the more I worked out, the more energy my body had and the more I wanted to work out. When I stopped working out, my body became accustomed to being lazy and wanted more rest and relaxation. The key was to form the best habits to help my body stay consistent in boosting my immune system.

**Improves eyesight**

After chemotherapy, I noticed an extreme change in my eyesight. It was not as sharp as it previously was. I had to squint more and adjust my eyes to see simple things. Someone suggested that I intensify my workout to help with my weight and eyesight. I learned that making exercise a regular part of your daily life can do wonders for your eyes. Regular exercise can help prevent macular degeneration, cataracts, glaucoma, and other eye problems. It can also improve the visibility of your vision by decreasing the thickness of your cataracts and your overall cataract health. If you have diabetes, high blood pressure, or other health problems that affect eye muscles, ask your doctor before starting an exercise regimen. Note that exercise is not a replacement for seeing a medical professional and not designed to replace your glasses. Exercise is simply an additional resource to help improve and maintain your health and eyesight.

## It makes your bones stronger

From small children to adults, exercise can help make our bones stronger. If you have osteoporosis, regular exercise can help protect your bones from fracture. If you are a child, exercise can help you develop stronger bones. Exercise helps keep your bones strong and your blood circulating throughout your body, no matter your age. Exercise can also reduce the chance of falls in seniors and youth by improving balance and preventing fatigue. The more we use and activate our bones through exercise, the stronger they will become.

## It decreases the risk of depression

I often take a walk or work out when my mind is cluttered, I'm stressed, or feeling down. Regular exercise has been shown to reduce depression, and it may also help improve the quality of your sleep. When I work out, my body has released a lot of stored energy that leads to better rest. Exercise reduces the amount of time your brain spends on the task of simply thinking about sad or scary things. Working out gives us an escape from the low vibrating thoughts that can be harmful to our health. When your brain is not focusing on anything negative, you can achieve your goal of completing your daily tasks with less stress. Exercise is a proven mental health booster. Regular exercise can increase your confidence, your energy, and your self-esteem. I have added working out as part of my mental health plan. The benefits are endless and sometimes, going for a walk or working out allows me the space I need to clarify my feelings so I can be my own best coach.

## It can protect against kidney cancer

When I first found out I had cancer, I immediately thought about my kidneys and the issues I have had with them over the years. I was always prone to kidney stones. I also knew about the link between diabetes and kidney issues. Even if you do not have diabetes, kidney cancer is more common in smokers, but it's also more common in obese people. As I researched cancer to develop a plan to fight back, I found several links between excess weight and kidney cancer. The connection has been confirmed in several studies. As someone who is vulnerable to kidney issues, I increased my exercise levels and maintained a healthy weight as a way of protecting my kidneys.

## It can slow aging

Looking back at my high school and college classmates, it's not hard to tell who has taken care of themselves and who has not. I can even see it in myself. I lost forty pounds and got a haircut and people said it looked as if I was aging in reverse. Exercise has been shown to help slow the rate of aging in several ways. It can enhance circulation, reduce body fat, protect you from the effects of aging, and keep your muscles strong. In fact, exercise is helpful in keeping your muscles healthy. This is great news for older adults who want to live an active lifestyle. If you want to slow the impact of aging, safely introduce or increase exercise.

## Types of exercise

There are a variety of exercises to match any personality and fitness goals. The key is to find what works best for you. It is possible to do an activity that is beneficial to your physical and mental health while also ensuring it isn't physically harmful or increasingly difficult for you. You can also intensify your workout to find more aggressive goals. Below is a list of popular, less-intense exercises that can be done at home:

*High Intensity Interval Training*

While I was at my Cancer Treatment program in Eden's Valley, we focused on HIIT workouts. Our trainer, Carlos, who was in his mid 70s, was an amazing instructor as he guided and taught us all about this type of exercise. HIIT involves extreme exercises for short periods of time with periods of recovery in between. The work intervals are designed to be challenging and a push to your maximum effort. While completing these exercises, my goal was to increase periods of hard work and implement shorter breaks between. I urge you to find and determine your goals and create your own plan. You can do sprints and take a break. You could do planks, squats, leg lifts, and take breaks between each set. This is different from walking or jogging long distances where you are trying to balance your energy. In HIIT, you go as hard as you can then recover over and over again. It is particularly valuable if you don't have a lot of time to work out.

HIIT: By Carlos from Eden Valley Wellness Institute

The goal: Moderate muscle endurance and cardiovascular strength.

Milestone (a) 150 minutes total per week.

Milestone (b) incorporate 20-minute morning walk

Intense burst of activity + recovery period = 1 interval

Example of HIIT is as follows:

a. Warmup 5-7 minutes with an easy jog or walk.

b. 30 seconds controlled fast pace or speed walk near maximum effort

c. 2-3 minutes of easy walking to catch your breath

d. Repeat this process 8 to 10 times.

e. Cool down 5-7 minutes with an easy walk and some common stretches.

## Strength Training

Moreover, strength training is a great way to work your muscles. This type of activity works the muscles and builds strength. You can do it alone or in a class, and your exercise schedule can change as your body needs. The longer you exercise, the more muscle you will build. At the beginning, you may do strength training once a week. You will be surprised at how much better you will feel after you exercise for just a little while a few days a week.

## Cardiovascular Exercise

Cardiovascular exercise is another type of exercise that works your entire body. You will get a lot faster, and you will burn more calories with this type of exercise. While you won't run a marathon or play like a professional athlete, you may find that you can finish your favorite activity before you even realize it. You will build up endurance to do more. You may even find that an exercise that was previously difficult is now much easier for you to complete. You will be able to surprise your friends and colleagues when you show up to the track or court with more energy and endurance.

*Dance*

Additionally, dancing is a great way to exercise and boost your mood. I dance almost every day. I might not be good at it, but I feel good doing it. You don't have to go to a club or a party to do this. You can create your own party at any time. Try to find something that makes you want to move. Find a video online, do a social media challenge, or just be silly with family and friends. Whatever method you choose, find something that motivates you to move. You can have fun, boost your mood, and get exercise in at the same time.

The older you are, the greater the benefits of exercise seem to be. If you have heart or lung problems, you will be more limited in what types of exercise you can do, so check with your doctors before engaging in new exercises and be cautious. You can also be more likely to experience an injury if you push yourself too hard. Self-awareness is key.

Currently, we all need to find exercises that can be done at home so we will have more options. You should do exercises at a time that is convenient for you and that does not disrupt your daily schedule. You should consult your doctor, trainer, or coach to determine the types of exercise that are most effective for you.

Whether you decide you need to walk, run, or dance, the key is to keep your body moving. You may want to try yoga, aerobics, or tai chi. These types of exercises use the same muscles as weightlifting, but are much less intense. There are a variety of tools and resources available for free online and through social media. Take advantage of the communities that already exist and find a place where you can get the fellowship that pushes you to the next level.

**Exercise Summary & Game Plan – Track your progress**
Why exercise?

- Exercise aids in the digestive process.

- It helps blood circulation.

- Helps get oxygen into the body, which improves respiration.

- Exercise helps build bone and muscle while also relaxing nerves.

- Exercise rejuvenates the mind while boosting the immune system and resistance to disease.

- Exercise helps maintain weight, health, and beauty.

What is your plan for getting your weekly exercise.

Fitness Goals

| Start Date: | Start Weight: | Start BMI: |
|---|---|---|
| Duration: | Goal Weight: | Goal BMI: |
| End Date: | End Weight: | End BMI: |

| Motivation | Action plan |
|---|---|
| What is your motivation for this goal? | What is the plan to accomplish this goal? |
| **Good Habits to Start** | **Bad Habits to Stop** |

# WORKOUT PLAN

| | ACTIVITY | TIME | REPS |
|---|---|---|---|
| **DAY 1** | • Record 3 Activities Below<br>• 1<br>• 2<br>• 3 | 20 min<br>10 min<br>2 hrs. | 5 times<br>10 reps<br>1 round |
| **DAY 2** | • Record 3 Activities Below<br>• 1<br>• 2<br>• 3 | 20 min<br>10 min<br>2 hrs. | 5 times<br>10 reps<br>1 round |
| **DAY 3** | • Record 3 Activities Below<br>• 1<br>• 2<br>• 3 | 20 min<br>10 min<br>2 hrs. | 5 times<br>10 reps<br>1 round |
| **DAY 4** | • Record 3 Activities Below<br>• 1<br>• 2<br>• 3 | 20 min<br>10 min<br>2 hrs. | 5 times<br>10 reps<br>1 round |
| **DAY 5** | • Record 3 Activities Below<br>• 1<br>• 2<br>• 3 | 20 min<br>10 min<br>2 hrs. | 5 times<br>10 reps<br>1 round |

# Water

When I first moved to Phoenix from Atlanta, one of the main adjustments I had to make was the extreme change in temperature and the climate between the 2 cities. Atlanta is a very humid city and Phoenix is hot and dry. Over the course of the first summer in the city, I found myself feeling a bit off. I was feeling sick at first, but then I started getting strange pains that would come and go. One day while I was at work, I got really sick. I was in pain and had to leave. I went to the urgent care, and they found out that I was extremely dehydrated. As a result of my chronic dehydration, I had developed kidney stones. I had to start a hydration routine to rehydrate my body and pass the kidney stone.

Fast forward about 10 years to when I was working as a high school teacher. I was so busy on most days that I didn't even take a restroom break until lunch or even after school. As a result, I also cut back on the amount of water and fluids I was taking in. I began to sip flavored carbonated water for the taste and not for appropriate hydration. It was not long before the chronic hydration set in, and the kidney stones returned.

This was a reoccurring theme in my life for the better part of a decade. I would go through periods of extreme dehydration followed by kidney stones, and as a result, other issues followed. I still find myself struggling to stay on top of my hydration goals but it's a journey that requires attention and focus, and one that I am more than willing to embark on.

There are a tremendous number of benefits from drinking water and staying hydrated. Water reduces the risk of heart attack, helps you maintain an ideal weight, reduced blood pressure and cholesterol. Many other diseases such as kidney stones, high blood pressure, gallbladder disease, constipation, and urinary tract infections can be treated with the intake of water in recommended amounts. Studies show that drinking more than 5 glasses of water reduces the risk of death from coronary heart disease. In fact, drinking water is better for overall health than consuming any other beverages, such as tea, coffee, soft drinks, and fruit juices.

It is important to stay hydrated. I found out firsthand that dehydration causes blood clotting, dizziness, headaches, tiredness, and dry mouth. To help stay hydrated, drink one glass of water after you wake up, and one glass before you go to sleep. I usually try to stop drinking about an hour or so before going to sleep, which has been shown to reduce the risk of heart attack during sleep. The recommended amount of water, in ounces, that you should drink every day, is half of your body weight in pounds. For example, I weigh about 200 pounds, so I should be drinking about 100 ounces of water per day at minimum. Do the math for your body weight and create a plan for the day. Also, your body needs more water if you have a fever, after you exercise, or in warmer temperatures in which you sweat a lot. If you naturally sweat like me, you might want to increase the recommended amount of water intake.

Here are some evidence-based health benefits of staying hydrated:

**Improves physical performance**

Regardless of whether you are a high performing athlete or a working professional, being and staying hydrated is vital. It is common for athletes to lose as much as 2-10% of their water weight via sweat, which can lead to increased fatigue and reduced motivation. When this happens, the athlete cannot maintain the exercise any longer. However, if you stay hydrated, you can perform at your absolute best.

**Prevents joint pain**

Most of our body is made of water. This includes the cartilage in joints, which contains 80% water. It is believed that there are over 350 joints in the human body. When the body is dehydrated, all of them are deprived of the primary resource they need: water. Drinking enough water lubricates the joints and maintains their shock-absorbing ability. When you are dehydrated, their shock absorbing ability decreases, leading to potential pain in a variety of spots throughout your body.

**Reduces stress**

When I get dehydrated, I noticed that I get a headache and become increasingly frustrated. When your body is dehydrated, the brain senses this and sends a signal to release cortisol, a hormone that promotes feelings of stress and anxiety. Your body then becomes off balance. However, being adequately hydrated restores the hormone levels and reduces stress. You are able to think more clearly and give your organs the vital resource they need, which helps reduce stress in the body overall.

**Reduces the risk of blood clots**

I had a history of blood clots in my family which led me to do more research on their cause and impact. I found that dehydration causes the blood to become thicker, which leads to high blood pressure. Also, blood is 90% water, and is responsible for carrying oxygen to different parts of the body. When the body is dehydrated, there is a direct impact on the blood in the body. It is extremely important for your body to maintain its water balance.

**Keeps blood sugar levels in control**

When I was told about my cancer and pre-diabetic status, I immediately cut out all sugary drinks and juices. My focus was on drinking lemon water. I realized that it is important to drink water to help maintain proper blood glucose levels. I could see a definitive difference in my bloodwork when I was drinking water and staying hydrated compared to when I was drinking juice and not following a hydration plan. In fact, staying hydrated is one of the best ways to prevent and manage diabetes, which is why so many people are looking for a way to manage diabetes without medication. I did it with diet, exercise, and hydration, which sheds light on the importance of these things for optimal health.

## Improves brain functioning

We need to stay hydrated because our brain is made up of up to 80% water. If your body is dehydrated, so is your brain. The brain is responsible for processing our daily thoughts. If it doesn't have the primary resources it needs, how can we be the best version of ourselves? We won't be able to function at our maximum mental ability because our bodies and brains are deficient in what they need to function.

The brain is also responsible for our balance and coordination; it helps us maintain good motor skills. When we are dehydrated, many of our daily functions are impacted. So, keeping hydrated helps us function at our maximum capacity. Hydration provides our bodies with energy and prevents feelings of hunger and fatigue allowing us to maximize ourselves.

## Stimulates the immune system

Water is a key component to helping keep our body healthy. We need plenty of water to keep our immune system well-hydrated, helping to prevent infections and maintaining the health of our bodies. When we are dehydrated, the immune system can't function at its highest level, leaving us vulnerable to attacks and infections. A properly hydrated body will help keep our immune system performing well and fighting off disease and infection.

## Stimulates your metabolism

When I wake up in the morning, the first thing I do is drink a glass of water. I realized that often, when I feel hungry, I am actually just in need of water. When I am eating instead of drinking, I am not giving my body what it needs. The brain is the body's main regulator for maintaining metabolism and digestion. Without water, your entire system cannot function properly, and your diet will be unbalanced. When drinking the appropriate amount of water, you won't have the same desire to snack and eat unnecessarily. Water helps keep the body's temperature stable and its metabolic processes up to speed.

## Decreases mood swings and keeps you calm

Dehydration impairs your brain's ability to send and receive information and emotions. As such, it often leads to mood swings, irritability, depression, fatigue, stress, and anxiety. When we drink water and stay properly hydrated, we can settle our mood and emotions by helping the brain transmit information. I notice a difference in my mood when I am drinking liquids high in sugar versus water.

## Speeds up your recovery

Getting and keeping your body adequately hydrated helps speed up any recovery process. After an intense workout or race, most of us feel tired and dehydrated. Rehydrating will ensure our bodies are rested and rejuvenated for future exercise. Considering how much of our body is made of water, logically, we can see how drinking water is vital in aiding a recovering body. Whether it be recovering from a workout or a surgery, being properly hydrated is a huge asset.

**Provides your skin with the nutrients it needs**

Whenever I look in the mirror and I see skin irritations, I know that I have not been drinking the right amount of water. Our skin needs a lot of nutrients and minerals to maintain a healthy level of hydration and maintain its elasticity. Loose skin and wrinkles occur when the body lacks water. They form when the body's fluid levels drop and the fluid doesn't get replaced. When we drink and stay hydrated, we can see the glow and health of our skin. But when our body is dehydrated, we often start to look older and unhealthy.

**Improves circulation**

Water is vital in keeping our circulation at full capacity. When the blood flows properly, oxygen reaches the muscles and tissues of the body, speeding up the repair and rebuilding process. If our body is not properly hydrated, the circulation is impacted, which in turn impacts the body's ability to heal and repair.

## Improves sports performance and physical well-being

Getting the body hydrated after a strenuous workout helps reduce the risk of injury while also improving mood and energy levels. Also, sports enthusiasts and bodybuilders often get reminders to hydrate their muscles after exercise, especially when they experience muscle cramps and swelling. Despite our activity levels, we should adopt the same routine and ensure we are consistently staying hydrated.

## Regulate your digestive system

I believe that my chronic dehydration played a role in my cancer diagnosis. When I looked at the issues that dehydration causes in the digestive system, I saw a direct connection. If your body is not properly hydrated, then the toxins that should be flushed out sit inside your body longer than they should. This gives waste and toxins that should be passing through the opportunity to become part of your body, which could result in disease and illness.

It is important to stay hydrated so your digestive system can function properly and efficiently. Dehydration leads to acidity, digestive problems, constipation, and heartburn. We need to stay hydrated for the bowel to work properly.

Since the greater part of our bodies are made of water, our diet should be a closer reflection of our composition. The majority of people I know who are overweight are also dehydrated. If we created a hydration plan, many of the illnesses we face would begin to disappear, along with the obesity that is impacting our nation's health.

## Water Summary & Game Plan – Track your intake

Water is one of the most important factors in all our bodies' functions and processes. We often overlook a hydration plan as a vital part to our survival and health maintenance. One of the main issues contributing to dehydration is the confusion of thirst with hunger. We often consume dehydrating food when our bodies are calling for water. Having a water conscious mindset and a hydration plan must be a priority.

- When blood is low or lacking water, it takes what it needs from the skin.

- When the skin is lacking water, it takes from the liver.

- When the liver is lacking and low on water, it takes from the kidneys.

- When the kidneys are low or lacking water, they take from the colon.

Note that it is best to drink a half hour before meals and hour after meals, so the water is not diluting your digestive acids. Ideally, your meals would be served with no drinks.

**Hydration Plan**

| Wake Up | Drink 8 to 16 ounces to start your day |
|---------|----------------------------------------|
| Pre work | Drink 8 to 16 ounces prior to starting work |
| 1st Break | Drink 8 to 16 ounces during your first break |
| Lunch | Drink 8 to 16 ounces before lunch |

| Post Lunch | Drink 8 to 16 ounces 30 minutes to one hour after lunch |
| --- | --- |
| Afternoon break | Drink 8 to 16 ounces during break |
| Dinner | Drink 8 to 16 ounces before dinner |
| Last Sip | Drink 8 to 16 ounces one hour before bed |

Don't underestimate the value of having a hydration plan. Water is the foundation to life.

# DAILY WATER &HEALTH TRACKER

**GOAL:**

**B**
BREAKFAST

**L**
LUNCH

**D**
DINNER

**S**
SNACK

**EXERCISE:**

**CUPS OF WATER**

◯ ◯ ◯ ◯
◯ ◯ ◯ ◯

**AFFIRMATIONS:**

YdrateNelson.com

# Sunshine

Prior to my introduction to NEW START, I never would have considered sunshine as a law of health. In essence, the sun is the greatest gift of life. From encouraging the development of plants and other fruits to helping individuals stay warm, sunlight is a prerequisite for life in every aspect. Without the sun, there is no life. I love the feeling of sunlight against my skin, but beyond the beams lie ample health benefits. Evidence suggests that sunlight provides numerous health benefits.

Before we go and overdose on sunshine, it's important to remember the potential risk. Many people are cautious when it comes to an increased amount of exposure to the sun, as high levels of UV radiation can lead to skin cancer. It is essential that individuals protect themselves from an increased amount of exposure to sunlight. All things in moderation. However, ensure that you still get enough sunlight to enjoy its health benefits. If you can get the right amount of sunlight, you will be able to better absorb vitamin D and all the health benefits that come with it.

When I was first diagnosed with cancer, I met with a naturopathic doctor as part of my treatment team with the CTCA. As we reviewed my bloodwork, he pointed out my vitamin D levels and asked if I was aware of my deficiency. He told me that he had seen a direct correlation between vitamin D levels and mortality. I was shocked when I discovered that my vitamin D levels were so low because I was living in Arizona, and we get the most sunshine in the country. The truth is, even though the sun is shining outside, it doesn't mean we're getting the appropriate amount of sunshine our bodies need.

At that point, I realized that sunshine alone wasn't going to help me get my levels where they needed to be. I found natural supplements and started taking them daily. I also added sunbathing to my diet as part of my treatment program. I studied the benefits of vitamin D in the human body so I could better understand how I was being impacted.

I found a connection between vitamin D deficiency and cancer.

## Health Benefits of Sunlight
### *Physical health benefits*

Skin, bones, eyes, and the brain all need sun for optimal performance.

One of the primary health benefits of getting the right amount of sunlight is the use of skin in the production of vitamin D in the body. When we're exposed to sunlight as UV rays hit our skin, it works with the 7 DHC protein right beneath the skin to aid in the production of vitamin D3. When we don't get enough sunshine, this process is circumvented, thus leading or contributing to a deficiency in vitamin D. In one of the NEW START lectures, I was taught that vitamin D is known as the anti-cancer vitamin because it can stop cancer cells from running, while also potentially converting them back to normal cells. In my case, my vitamin D levels were bottomed out and the cancer was spreading throughout my body. My first attack on cancer was to increase my vitamin D levels.

In addition to sun, people can get their fair share of vitamin D through a balanced diet and health supplements. Vitamin D is an essential nutrient for our body to initiate and break down of other chief biological processes that take place in and outside of the body. Vitamin D also helps with the assimilation of calcium in the body, providing several benefits, including:

- Promoting healthy bones

- Elevating calcium levels

- Reducing amounts of inflammation

- Managing the immune system and metabolism

That being said, there is a relationship between sun exposure and decreased levels of blood pressure. The byproduct results in lower death rates associated with heart attacks and cardiac complications simply by spending time with mother nature. It has been proven that exposure to sunlight can assist the skin and help the arteries to dilate, which in turns lowers blood pressure levels. Other research suggests that sun exposure may also prevent and treat several diseases, including colon cancer, breast cancer, prostate cancer, and non-Hodgkin lymphoma.

According to researchers, those who live in areas with fewer daylight hours are more likely to have some specific cancers than those who live where there is more sun during the day. These cancers include:

- Colon cancer

- Pancreatic cancer

- Prostate cancer

- Hodgkin's lymphoma

- Ovarian cancer

According to the World Health Organization (WHO), sun exposure can also help treat several skin conditions such as:

- Psoriasis

- Eczema

- Jaundice

- Acne

Consulting a dermatologist is recommended as light therapy isn't for everyone, although for many, it will benefit their specific skin concerns. The WHO suggests getting anywhere from 5 to 15 minutes of sunlight on your arms, hands, and face 2-3 times a week. If you are going to be outside for more than 15 minutes, it's recommended to protect your skin by wearing a protective shirt, hat, and proper attire.

### *Mental health benefits*

Moreover, being out in the sun generally makes people feel good, and there are many scientific reasons as to why this happens. One of those reasons is that exposure to UV rays causes the skin to produce beta-endorphins, which are hormones that reduce pain. Sunlight also has a direct relationship with mental health. When an individual's skin receives a healthy dose of sunlight, then the person is likely to experience the same effects on their own mental and physical health.

People who soak up increased amounts of sunlight are often associated with individuals who are more emotionally stable, whereas more mental distress is found in people who get little or no sun exposure. Exposing yourself to increased amounts of sunlight also increases serotonin levels in the human body that can help people suffering from anxiety, depression, and other mental ailments. Furthermore, researchers also claim that getting sunlight exposure in the day can help improve your sleeping patterns during the night. This may also help people diagnosed with insomnia.

Other benefits of sunlight and vitamin D include:

- Relieving pain

- Helping wounds heal

- Helping people feel more alert

- Boosting the immune system

- Reducing depression

- Improving overall mental health

Thus, sunlight is not only beneficial for our physical health, but it also impacts our mental health. There have been plenty of days when I was at work or home and felt moody, frustrated, and even depressed. Going outside and getting some sun can change your mood within minutes. If it beneficial for your mind and mood, it will also benefit you physically, and vice versa. If sunshine has been part of your lifestyle, continue to expose yourself to it moderately to avoid overexposure. If it has not been part of your lifestyle, create a way to integrate it into your daily life. Check your vitamin D levels to make sure you don't have deficiencies.

**Sunshine Game Plan – Track your intake**

Sunshine is a valuable part of our daily diet that often gets overlooked. To avoid deficiencies caused by a lack of sun, we need to understand the importance of it and develop a plan accordingly.

- Getting the right amount of sunshine can help lower blood pressure, reduce stress, and improve feelings of depression.

- Sunshine is a natural source of vitamin D which helps maintain healthy bones by aiding the body in absorbing calcium from food sources. If you have a deficiency in vitamin D, soy, almonds, and rice, beverages are a good supplementary source.

## Coaching Support Questions

1.  How much sunshine do you get daily?

2.  Do you need to allocate more time in your schedule to spend outside? How do you plan on increasing your sunshine intake?

3.  Do you know your vitamin deficiencies?

4.  What is your maintenance plan moving forward to address adequate sunshine needs and potential deficiencies?

## Recommended Actions

- Exercising outside with appropriate protection for extremities is a great way to stay fit and get some sunshine.

- Sleep in areas that are open to sunlight.

- Try to go for a walk daily. Even 5 minutes will help.

- Stand facing the sun with your eyes closed for short periods of time.

# SUN TRACKER

TRACK THE DAYS YOU SPEND 10 MINUTES OR MORE IN THE SUN:

MONTH OF: _____

|  | S | M | T | W | T | F | S |
|---|---|---|---|---|---|---|---|
| **WEEK ONE** | | | | | | | |
| **WEEK TWO** | | | | | | | |
| **WEEK THREE** | | | | | | | |
| **WEEK FOUR** | | | | | | | |

**NOTES**

# Temperance

Temperance is the foundation to great health. Temperance is defined as having virtuous qualities, such as having respect for oneself and others, moderation regulating emotions, non-violence, honesty, and compassion. In other words, temperance is about infusing the things that make life peaceful into your mindset. Essentially, it means saying no to the bad and moderating the good.

In modern times, this approach has taken the form of abstinence from alcohol and many other vices. From this perspective, temperance means abstaining from behaviors which create conflict, negative emotions, or suffering.

In the health realm, temperance is saying no to things that are harmful and practicing moderation in the things that are good and beneficial. Too much of anything can be a bad thing. As much as we need sun and water, even they can become harmful if too much is consumed. Some people can get sunburns or even cancer from long exposure to the sun.

Drinking too much water could cause pressure in the skull and in extreme cases, even lead to death. This validates that we need moderation in all things. This has been a struggle for me personally and has contributed to my health demise in the past.

There was a point when I would do and eat whatever I wanted. I overindulged in drinking and ate like a king. I didn't gage myself; I just did what mentally felt and tasted good to me. I didn't have a nutrition plan or any type of system in place to ensure my body was balanced. My weight spiraled out of control along with my health. Even after I was initially warned by my doctor, I kept doing whatever felt good.

In my youth, I maintained terrible lifestyle choices. My youth and energy kept up appearances of health, but those habits were not sustainable in the long-run. By the time I hit my late 30s and early 40s, I noticed my previous lifestyle choices coming back to haunt me. My inability to say no to the things that were harming me and moderate the things I loved was killing me. Embracing temperance became a matter of life and death.

We tend to tend to think of temperance as a virtue that one can cultivate and strengthen. Often, temperance can be thought of as a passive thing, where one does things that are in line with a general rule of good behavior. It's helpful to understand that temperance is more proactive than passive. When people drink, they become intolerant, hostile, and in some cases, overall bad people. When people lie, they become unkind, vengeful, and self-serving. So, if we are drinking, lying, and being vengeful, we are practicing things that are contrary to our principles of temperance. I have found that it is often harder to not do something than it is to do it. That is not passive at all. It requires focus and discipline developed through a tempered mind.

When I think about eating my favorite desserts and foods that are not nutritious and will not serve my body, saying no is often harder than giving into my desires. Not doing something in this case is harder than doing it. However, my habits make it easy for me to give in to my desires. I am always in search of a way to reinforce my mindset and become more tempered in this regard.

This is where spiritual mindfulness and meditation come in. When we practice temperance at a high level, we are actively practicing these things in a new way and creating new habits. We are increasing our capacity to cultivate the strengths of our body, mind, and heart. We are creating new qualities in ourselves, which will foster better, more peaceful relationships with others, improve our sense of wellbeing, and reduce the suffering we are experiencing in our lives.

In the same way, temperance is a discipline that can be practiced in and of itself. The more we can cultivate the physical, mental, and emotional components of temperance, the more we will manifest the good health, beauty, and peace that it is all about. In other words, temperance is the seed that enables compassion to bloom, leading to more compassionate relationships, more spiritual awareness, and greater inner peace. This lifestyle emphasizes reaching and maintaining optimal health.

In short, temperance is the foundation of spirituality and superior health. So, if we want to cultivate the spiritual qualities of mindfulness, contemplation, compassion, pure awareness, appreciation, and reflection, we must first learn to cultivate our body, mind, and heart. Our body, mind, and heart are the 3 major components of being spiritually healthy and happy.

That being said, if we are conscious of the tools we use to create and manifest, we can create those things. One example is through the development of mindfulness. If we develop our mindfulness to the point where we can savor and enjoy every moment, we will be able to concentrate on what we do to create, feel, and express our lives in a more meaningful and fulfilling way. We will create a life that is more conducive to those qualities we want, rather than simply living out of fear or desperation. Living in fear and operating in survival mode is detrimental to our overall health.

For better health, it is necessary that we show temperance in all things. That includes temperance in what we eat, drink, wear, and do. Having what seems to be moderation in all things helps maintain good health. I have noticed, however, that some people cannot tolerate temperance in some areas, even though they are able to carry it out in other areas.

Since temperance includes a commitment to uphold principles of goodness, some people feel that it is not a proper priority in their lives. They don't want to live by the principles of temperance, and are willing to compromise these principles to do what they want to do. They don't have the courage to be consistent with their lifestyle, and so they seek compromise in other areas of their lives, too. This was me before I was diagnosed with cancer. I was forced to reevaluate my entire mindset around my health and make tough decisions. It was not easy then and it is not easy now. It's a daily journey with wins and losses. The marathon continues.

Temperance is the secret to good health. It is the means of preventing suffering and its consequences. It's easy to say we should avoid doing things that bring suffering and conflict. But it's another thing to realize that we need to do that, and then do it.

I can't tell you how many people I see suffering from eating disorders, or other disordered behaviors. They believe that some behaviors are healthy, and that others are not. They think they can eat what they like and never be overweight.

They are confused and sometimes angry with themselves for not living up to their expectations. This was also me. I was dominated by a lack of focus and discipline that played a role in my overall health and wellness.

We should all live according to our own principles, not based on other people's values. When we accept a principle, we are in no position to accept any exceptions. We are clear on our own individual convictions. We are not confused about ourselves, and we know what we should and shouldn't do. Again, it comes back to execution. Knowing what we should do and doing it are 2 completely different things. This is a journey with no particular destination. We are all a work in progress.

I believe that everyone should practice moderation in their behavior, but some people have trouble accepting this basic and inherent value. Our society overindulges in just about everything. I would like to propose a change. It is time that we become willing to accept the wisdom of temperance as the guiding principle of living. It is time that we do all things in moderation and minimize the things that don't serve us.

Those who are overweight, out of shape, or struggle with any other condition are suffering. We are all trying to live according to our own principles, and these principles may or may not be in harmony with a generalized idea of how to live our best life. We may or may not have the tools and resources to do this, and some of us may or may not feel strong enough to follow our convictions. We see this particularly in times of self-doubt.

If you can master temperance, mastering the other laws of health will be much easier. Temperance is all about your mindset and how focused and disciplined you are. If your mindset is focused on a goal and you are disciplined, there is nothing that can stop you from achieving said goal. You have a choice. You can master temperance on your own and move forward or deal with the back-end repercussions and dilemmas.

**Temperance Game Plan – Track your mindset.**

"Moderation in all things healthful; total abstinence from all things harmful."

- Get a diary or journal and write down your thoughts over the course of a day. Set an alarm for 3 different times and journal during that time. Put aside 5 to 10 minutes to journal.

## Coaching Support Questions

1. What are some things in your lifestyle that are not serving you or your health?

2. What can you do to change these lifestyle habits?

3. What are some of the good habits that will increase the quality of your life long-term?

4. What can you stop doing today that will help you tomorrow?

5. What are some things you can start doing right now that can benefit you long-term?

## Health Recommendations

Minimize at least all forms of alcohol and unnecessary drugs. The same applies to beverages like coffee, tea, and any soft drinks that contain caffeine.

- Use natural substances in place of over-the-counter medications. Avoid street drugs.

- Cut down on juices and soda while increasing water intake.

- Fast 2 back-to-back days per week. Determine what you are fasting from and the days you will be fasting. Once the time is set, be consistent.

- Cut processed and fermented foods and increase fruits and vegetables.

The first step to taking control of your health is taking control of your mind. When your mind and habits are consistently tempered, you will maximize your health.

**MORNING**

**TODAY'S MANTRA:**

.............................................................
.............................................................

**LOOKING FORWARD TO:**

.............................................................
.............................................................
.............................................................

**TO MAKE TODAY GREAT, I WILL:**

.............................................................
.............................................................
.............................................................

**EVENING**

**I AM GRATEFUL FOR:**

.............................................................
.............................................................

**PEOPLE I APPRECIATE:**

.............................................................
.............................................................
.............................................................

**THREE GOOD THINGS TODAY:**

.............................................................
.............................................................
.............................................................

**OTHER THOUGHTS**

**MOMENT TO REMEMBER**

# HABIT TRACKER

WEEK OF: _____

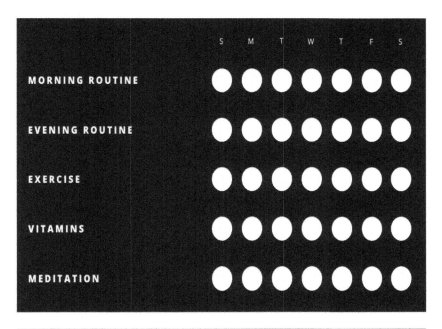

NOTES

# Air

My personal goal to walk 10,000 steps per day is not only beneficial for exercise and sunshine, but also for getting fresh air. Since I was diagnosed with cancer, I added air to my daily diet. Whether it's taking a walk, exercising outside, or taking my kids to the park, I've prioritized conscious air in my life.

Obviously, fresh air is incredibly important for breathing purposes and contains all the required oxygen levels important for survival. As we see, fresh air is important for the transfer of pollen in terms of reproduction and movement of water molecules in the form of gases from one place to another, which can be one of the fundamentals of the water cycle. But that's another topic the former science teacher in me can discuss later. What we need to discuss here is how fresh air can benefit our mental and physical health.

I, like many people, found myself working in offices for almost 70% of my life. From corporate jobs to restaurants and to schools, the average person spends a huge chunk of their day inside. This makes them unable to get the fresh air they need, and it stops them from getting intimate with nature. Such people who sit behind the desk all day may experience psychological disorders and may face more difficulties than those who receive fresh air regularly.

## The Covid-19 Scare

During a pandemic, we see that people are not getting the right amount of fresh air. People have their faces hidden under different kinds of masks and many are afraid to take them off for fear of being infected by the deadly virus. Still, people take out time during the pandemic to get fresh air. Assuming safe distances between yourself and others can help you get the fresh air your body needs.

## Importance of being outside

During the pandemic, people have resorted to outdoor exercise because it may be dangerous to head to a gym. People should resort to sports such as hiking, swimming, biking, running, and even canoeing. Most of these exercises can be done individually and can help you get the fresh air you need.

With a combination of a pandemic and a boom in technology, it is unsurprising that many people are stuck inside a room with a very narrow-minded approach to everything involving the outside world. Many people are experiencing depression or pandemic fatigue and feel difficulty roaming outside and talking to people outside their bubble. However, it is still vital to engage with nature and get fresh air. The following are some of the main benefits of being outside and breathing fresh air:

## Health purpose

Fresh air has been known to add value to a healthy lifestyle. It helps in regulating metabolism and digesting food in less time, which works against the accumulation of extra fat on the body. Fresh air helps lower blood pressure, helps maintain it at normal levels, and helps keep the heart rate at an appropriate pace. Moreover, it works in reducing obesity because walking in fresh air reduces body fat. It also helps in strengthening the immune system. This is because when you face healthy pathogens, they help strengthen the immune system. Walking outside with your family in fresh air helps strengthen family ties because it makes you follow a healthy lifestyle while forming healthy habits.

## Happiness guaranteed

Heart problems are a leading cause of death in almost all countries over the globe. Now, when you are happy, you are less prone to such problems. This happiness is brought on by the fresh air that we inhale when we walk outside in the bed of nature. According to recent studies, positive emotions are associated with healthy lifestyle habits. These higher levels of feel-good emotions are brought about when a person doesn't smoke, has good physical exertion, has better quality of sleep, and has access to vitamins.

## Detoxification of lungs

For detoxifying lungs, the first thing we need to do is stop smoking and expose ourselves less to dust and other consequences of air pollution. Only after that can the fresh air help in constricting and dilating the airways and improving the cleaning action of the lungs. It is said that when you inhale and exhale through your lungs, you remove airborne waste and toxins from your body.

## Sharpness of mind and energetic lifestyle

When we look at research conducted in the past, we discover that when we inhale fresh air and are surrounded by nature, our energy levels increase to a 90%. There is always a positive effect of being outside, being in the proximity of nature, and inhaling fresh air. I can see a difference personally when I get out and nature versus the days when I'm inside little fresh air or sunshine.

## Disadvantage/Lack of Fresh Air

When our bodies don't receive enough fresh air, our brains receive a reduced level of oxygen, thus causing a variety of issues, including:

- Fatigues

- Dizziness

- Poor decision making

- Dullness of mind

- Irritation from small talks

- Nausea

- The following are good habits to implement in this regard:

- Opening windows and curtains to let in sunlight

- Avoiding the use of chemical based air fresheners and cleansers

- Adding live plants to the house to help absorb toxins. Some plants like dracaenas, golden pothos, and peace lilies can be beneficial.

In short, fresh air is very beneficial, specifically in trying times like a pandemic. The coronavirus has reduced the intake of fresh air due to the need for masks in public spaces. People are saving themselves from infections and resort to being indoors. Now that there are vaccines against the microbe and people can reduce infections by maintaining safe distances, there is a golden chance for people to return to their normal lifestyles and get more and more fresh air into their systems.

## Fresh Air Game Plan – Just Breathe

Getting fresh air is the foundation of life. Without air, there is no life.

## Coaching Support Questions

1. How often do you practice deep breathing exercises?

2. How much time are you spending in nature? Do you need more?

3. How do you plan to increase your fresh air intake?

4. What are some things that you do that harm your ability to maintain fresh air intake?

5. Who else in your circle needs to increase their fresh air intake? How can you support each other?

# NOTES

## Breathing Recommendations

- Try some deep breathing exercises. Inhale deeply, count to ten, exhale, and hold for 10 seconds. Repeat 3 to 4 times a day.

- Avoid inhaling smoke, pollutants, damp musty odors, mold, or anything harmful to your lungs and body.

- Keep circulation and fresh air around the area where you sleep.

- Walk at least 5,000 steps each day outside.

Sometimes the best thing we can do is step back and just take a deep breath. If we have fresh air in our lungs, there is nothing we can't accomplish. Just breathe.

# NOTES

# Rest

"Rest your body, calm your spirit, restore your mind, and soothe your soul."

I used to wear sleep deprivation like a badge of honor. In my 20s, I hustled all night long in the studio. As an adult, I stayed up late working on assignments for my master's degree until the early morning. As a parent of young children, we're up in the middle of the night for a season tending to newborns. Many of my peers also take pride in working and staying up for long hours. They say it's a blessing and a virtue to work hard and earn an honest living, to wake up at dusk and go to work to earn a livelihood. However, too much of a good thing can be a bad thing. As important as it is to earn a living and improve your loved ones' lives, it is also important to get enough rest and sleep.

Without rest, you are putting all your hard work in danger and risking making things harder. The main purpose of earning money and attaining facilities is to make your life easier. But if you are engrossed in physical and mental turmoil all day, no amount of money or work can stop the irreversible detrimental effects on your health. In doing so, it is of utmost importance that you work but also relax. As we've already discussed, creating a healthy balance is key.

Integrating rest into my routine came when I was recovering from surgery. I had to remind myself that rest was an essential part of my healing and without the proper amount, my body would have a harder time recovering. As I worked on my recovery plan, I had to add in sleep and naps to allow my body the time it needed to heal. I was used to always going from event to event, but I had to slow things down to make rest a priority.

In time, I realized the vital need for rest, the benefits of getting it, and the dangerous impact of not getting it. Many times, we are doing damage without even realizing it. Below are a few of the benefits of rest to help you realize how important it is to take care of yourself.

**Benefits of Sleep**

Sleep is the best form of rest and can cure so many issues. When you drift off to sleep at the right time (usually at 9 or 10 pm) for at least 7 hours, your body's internal clock works well. Sleeping restfully allows our sleep-wake cycle to directly influence our body's essential functions. Circadian rhythms and sleep patterns directly affect some endogenous mechanisms. In turn, these endogenous systems influence glucose and lipid metabolism. Normal glucose and lipid metabolism are necessary to avoid life-endangering diseases like obesity, cardiovascular disease, hypertension, and cancer. So, it's more than imperative to get the needed rest and get a good night's sleep to avert these unwanted conditions. When you rest well, your bodily functions work well.

**Benefits of Naps**

Naps are short resting periods during the day that are taken to get rid of tiredness after a hectic work routine. It is a convenient and effective way to rest your body. This simple activity has so many positive outcomes, such as overall relaxation, reducing fatigue, and increasing alertness. Science says that napping during the day can be super effective for enhancing one's memory. It also increases our brain's activity so we can think better and quicker. Recently, research has revealed that taking naps 2 or 3 times a week can enhance heart health to avoid cardiovascular diseases and make you active and robust. After my surgery, I found that naps were a vital part to my recovery process. I added them to my lifestyle and try to get as many naps in as possible. It's not easy with 4 kids, but I have learned that every second counts.

## Benefits of Yoga

I discovered yoga when I moved to Phoenix. I bought a DVD and started having personal yoga sessions in my living room. Yoga is the act of both physical and mental endurance and is the perfect way to rest and relax one's mind and soul. Not only does it relax your mind, but it also calms your body of all the stress by releasing soothing hormones. This resting approach has all the positive outcomes that one can think of, from making you calmer to making you more alert. The easy and relaxed movements in yoga can ultimately make you more active in your day-to-day life. When you move your body in specific patterns, it causes the release of endorphins, dopamine, and serotonin, all of which are happy hormones. They make us feel lighter and more focused. You don't need to join a yoga studio to get started. There are plenty of books and YouTube videos that can guide you through the basics.

**Benefits of Meditation**

When we meditate, our mind is engrossed in the search for mental peace and serenity with a lesser contribution from our bodies, unlike yoga. It is an utmost requirement to keep our minds in a peaceful place so we can get the rest we need. With meditation, you will gain a new perspective on how to deal with difficult situations. If you meditate regularly, you will manage your stress better when you are well-rested. When you meditate, you rest your mind, and in turn, this gives you patience and tolerance. With this habit, it will be easier for you not to fall prey to negative emotions and thoughts and focus on what's most important in life.

## Benefits of Laying Down

You can rest your body and brain by lying down even if you're not sleeping or napping. This practice is much like meditation without any specific postures or movements involved. The goal is to rest all parts of your body, especially your brain. You don't have to focus on anything. You simply let any thoughts that come to your mind pass through. Give yourself and your body time to escape from everything. After lazily lying down alone, you will feel more connected to yourself. You will understand yourself better and be more self-aware and self-conscious.

## Benefits of listening to soothing music

Another way to rest your mind is to listen to soothing music. When you are indulged in a sweet melody, it triggers your mind to release happy hormones like serotonin and oxytocin that make you feel elevated and improve your mood. This activity will help you clear your head and get a better perspective on life. When you feel rested and calm, it improves your relationships with the people you love.

Relaxed and at ease, you can tackle difficult situations effectively and efficiently. A slow and unhurried melody will quiet your nervous system and help you get rid of every troublesome worry. This method of rest also eases muscle tension among many other benefits.

## Coaching Support Questions

1. How much rest do you normally get daily? How many hours of sleep do you get?

2. Are you currently resting enough? How can you get more rest?

3. What benefits will you gain from being more rested?

4. What will be the price you pay for not getting enough rest?

5. What is your rest strategy moving forward?

## Rest Recommendations

- **Get an adequate amount of sleep**. Most of us need at least 8 hours of sleep per night. Find a way to get some quiet time before going to bed. If you are having a hard time resting or sleeping, find a relaxing activity to do before bed. If you are reading, use a book over the electronic screen. Don't eat a big meal before bed. Try to sleep before midnight because pre-midnight hours are twice as restful as anything that comes after.

- **Exercise and work out**. Working out during the day will give you more endurance and improve stress management. Working out close to bedtime might give you unneeded energy. Find the perfect time and blend of activities for your lifestyle.

- **Engage in regular recreation and diversion**. Take every opportunity to take a vacation, trip, or a chance to see and do something different. Don't leave a second of vacation time. Spend time with friends and family. Hug your family and express your love. The feeling will bring you peace and allow you to relax.

**Final thoughts**

Lack of sleep affects us all in different ways, but none of them are positive. Our bodies are our treasures. Health is not expensive—it is priceless. Your health is your greatest wealth. It's all too easy to lose yourself in the race to get ahead in life, but it's also vital to take care of yourself and be fully rested so you can be there for your loved ones.

*We can not be so rushed to secure the money and bag and end up in a body bag. We must take time to rest and heal. Health is priceless.*

| DATE | TIME | WAKE UP TIME | BED TIME | TOTAL HOURS SLEPT |
|------|------|--------------|----------|-------------------|
|      |      |              |          |                   |

# Trust In Self & God

I am not a super religious person. I can't quote a ton of bible verses. You might not find me in church every Sunday, but I know and trust that there is a Higher Power that helps guide and direct my life. Have you ever wondered what keeps you safe, sane, and going despite all the wrongdoings and menaces we create with our health and life? I am confident that it is all because of the Most High, God. Faith helped me battle the biggest adversity of my life: stage 4 cancer.

There is no powerful force for human health other than having a deep and reflective trust in God. As a matter of fact, faith affects every dimension of our existence because God created us to be in communion with Him. I would often tell my doctors and physicians, you are not my primary doctor, God is.

The various dimensions of our life—be they physical, emotional, social, intellectual, or biochemical—are meant to be unified at the very core with a firm trust in God to help us find the meaning and direction in life. Being in tune with God is important for our physical well-being. It has also played a major role in my decision-making process during my most recent health battle. Believing in myself was essential, but my faith in a Higher Power gave me a level of faith I could not reach by just believing in myself.

When you are assured of God's approval and covering, it will impact your life in a valuable way, specifically in regard to your physical and mental health. It will fortify your soul against doubt, confusion, and trauma that often penetrate through our vital sources. Thus, the good news of God's loveliness is the most strengthening source for us.

Contrary to this, being out of sync with God's disposition harbors feelings of despair and guilt, thus, depriving us of health and happiness that we could otherwise enjoy. The feeling of stepping away from God's path without a sense of forgiveness paves the way for poor health. Full restoration of health is often possible when spiritual illness, grief, guilt, and remorse have been addressed.

The connection between spiritual needs and physical health is multifaceted. Patients who confidently called on God for His help were more serene when faced with complex medical procedures and physical ailments. Whilst patients who didn't establish a connection with God or weren't particularly religious were certain their illness was a direct result of God's vengeance. Before I stepped into the CTCA, I stopped and prayed to God. I never prayed for healing. I prayed for the strength to endure whatever God brought my way.

We all come across individuals who credit their life-threatening illnesses to God's retribution. They acknowledge their disobedience to God. This convinces them that God is punishing them with illness and depriving them of an eternal life. When I was faced with my illness, I had this as a crutch and option for my sickness. But I made a different decision. I felt in my heart that God blessed me with cancer as a test to show up as my greatest self.

We need to have a firm belief in God's limitless grace, forgiveness, and the relationship it has with our health and faith. If understood properly, faith has a deep-rooted connection with human health. But this relationship is easily tarnished. This danger of distortion is particularly great in communities where high standards of faith and practice are prevalent. Since the modern world is twisted and sinful, our health consequently paves the way for our demise.

I had to face the reality that my plan may not be God's plan. In my mind, I could have planned to be healed but God could have had another plan. I had to come to grips with the reality that God's will and my will may not be the same. One day, I had to accept the fact that even though I wanted to live, and God could heal me, I could also die. I had to face death head on, but my faith comforted and covered me because I knew I was protected no matter the outcome.

When we keep our faith in God, we understand who the author is of all blessings and their outcomes. When we don't focus on a Higher Power and a personal relationship, we may look upon disease and death as a proceeding from God, as a punishment imposed on account of sin. Hence, someone who has been inflicted upon by calamity and disease may be further burdened by the label of being a great sinner or a failure. In my battle with cancer, I have encountered these kinds of people. There is a huge difference between those who believe and those who don't, and it has nothing to do with religion.

Today we are on the doorstep of a cultural revolution that presents new opportunities. It showcases an insightful relationship between physical health and spiritual wellbeing. Doctors are looking upon the benefits of faith to heal their patients considering prayer as a powerful form of medicine. I use prayer as part of my healing process and to help me overcome some of my biggest mental challenges.

The society we live in is more secular than ever, but where is this new interest in spirituality and health stemming from? Why is so much attention being given to the wholesome power of health? Answers to these questions aren't easy. The human thirst for spirituality is hard to quench. But the most persuasive reason for the renaissance of interest in spirituality and physical health has been the result of scientific investigations. Countless studies are proving the affiliation between religiosity or spirituality and health, and most of these studies point towards a positive relationship. Before it was simply speculation, but now we have solid and concreate proof of the benefits of belief.

People of faith who have long believed in the benefits of spirituality may need little or no evidence or scientific research. But in the age we dwell in, science is the dominant force behind whatever we accept or reject. It is the approach taken by millions and it is the empirical evidence for the relationship between faith-based healthcare, too.

God teaches us that taking care of our physical wellbeing is a part of faithfulness to Him. Care for physical health is good for the mental and spiritual wellbeing, too, which is commonly referred to as a holistic approach to life. People should not only cater to the health benefits of spirituality, but also to the spiritual benefits of healthy living.

Without maintaining this balance between trust in God and health, the popular take on spirituality is nothing more than a magic spell—false and short-lived. While there is plenty of evidence from science over the health benefits of placing trust in God, this cannot be our reason to be faithful. Our faith and trust in God's mercy and grace are in response to His love. The concept of abiding by God's grace is our faithful response and indeed a gift from Him.

Religious practices and spiritual beliefs that are associated with more positive outcomes include seeking God's forgiveness and support. Moreover, the approach to view illness and calamity as an opportunity to connect with God and acknowledge personal responsibility to collaborate with God as an active partner is much needed. It is this kind of faith and trust in God that grooms our health and prepares us to serve others with empathy and kindness.

The same God that healed the lepers, made the crippled walk, caused the blind to see, raised the dead to life, sent angels to protect His loved men is here to heal you as well. Will you put your trust in God? Will you hand complete control of your life to the Most High? Will you surrender to God and allow Him to walk you through life? He wants to lead us to blissful healing. If this is what you want, there is no other way but to turn to God! This is the only reason I made it through my battle. I never stopped believing.

## Believe In And Trust Yourself

While it is vital to have faith in God, it is equally important to have faith in yourself.

One of my mentors said, "I know you are a man of faith but if you think God is coming to save you, you are going to die." It might sound harsh, but what he was telling me was that I had to have faith that what I was doing was going to be effective, but I still had to do the work. I knew that having faith alone wasn't good enough. I could pray all day, but if I didn't act, I would not get results. I realized that a huge part of my recovery was based on my mental capacity to stay faithful and believe in myself.

There were many different things I had to try in my cancer battle. If I didn't have faith in myself, I wouldn't have completed some of the hard and undesirable tasks I completed. My belief in God was vital, but my belief in myself was also a major key to my victory.

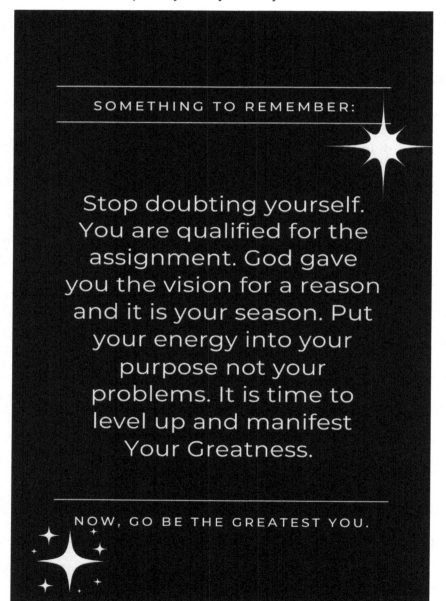

SOMETHING TO REMEMBER:

Stop doubting yourself. You are qualified for the assignment. God gave you the vision for a reason and it is your season. Put your energy into your purpose not your problems. It is time to level up and manifest Your Greatness.

NOW, GO BE THE GREATEST YOU.

# CHAPTER 1 - BELIEVE IN YOURSELF

## WHAT IS YOUR PLAN TO BUILD CONSISTENT CONFIDENCE IN YOURSELF?

Write it down.

## WHAT ARE YOUR THOUGHTS ABOUT YOURSELF AND YOUR ABILITIES?

Track your thoughts

## WHAT ARE YOUR STRENGTHS, WEAKNESSES, OPPORTUNITIES AND THREATS.

Write them out.

## WHO IS SUPPORTING YOU AND HELPING YOU STAY MOTIVATED?

1.Write them a thank you note and tell them exactly why you are thanking them.

# Conclusion

During this season of my life, I was tested in ways I never imagined. I was forced to evaluate my lifestyle and the decisions that contributed to my health. I was forced to take a NEW START because a pattern of unhealthy living impacted my health to the point that my life was on the line. I was looking death right in the face. My hope for you is that you are not forced to make extreme changes like I did. My hope is that you will be proactive and embrace a NEW START.

Taking on a NEW START is not a destination, it is a journey and a continued process. The process involves an intimate relationship between the mind and the body. They both are impacted by each other. If we truly desire to get on top of our health and life, then we need a balance between these 2 aspects. When we realize the degree that the mind impacts the body, we can create a mindset that aids our bodies in the healing process. Science has proven that many of the illnesses people face are a result of a negative mental state of depression. Our life forces are broken down when we deal with anger, guilt, discontent, anxiety, and distrust. They all impact our overall health.

When we are mentally battling something, it's hard to focus on making ensuring that we get the proper nutrition, exercise, and hydration we need. If we are not mentally prepared, we can't focus on getting sunshine, being tempered, maintaining fresh air supply, getting proper rest, and keeping faith in God. If we can focus on a NEW START, our minds won't be so distracted. Since many diseases are aggravated by negative thoughts and our imagination, controlling the invalid thoughts and creating a customized NEW START program can increase our health and prospects for longevity. We have the power. The ability to control our healing through our mind is in our hands.

When we apply the laws of health and combine them with faith, hope, courage, and love, we promote good health and prolong our life. Maintaining a positive mind and a cheerful spirit is a key component to optimal health. We are in a day and age where we have no excuse. We have the knowledge and the resources to maximize or health and wellness. Our time is now. We must maintain our physical and mental health to secure our legacies and maximize the time we have with our loved ones. We can control our health narrative. The power is in our hands. It's time to elevate our influence and leadership. What we do today will impact our legacies for generations to come. It's time to embrace a NEW START.

*No matter where you are in your journey, each day provides the opportunity for a NEW START. Embrace the process and enjoy the ride to optimal health.*

# About The Author

## Ydrate Nelson, M. Ed

Born and raised in Dublin, GA, Ydrate Nelson, M. Ed, AKA Ydrate The Motivator, is an award-winning humanitarian and **speaker,** poet, author, certified life **coach** and education **consultant**, who activates different techniques to engage, motivate, inspire, educate and empower audiences. Ydrate also has a passion for music and the arts and has several projects available on all music streaming services.

**Ydrate's Mission** is to be global leader in the motivation, coaching and education industries, building relationships on a passion for serving, living a motivated lifestyle and **striving for Greatness.**

Ydrate has over **20 years of professional experience** including high school and adult educator, management/leadership roles, marketing associate and financial recovery specialist. He has worked in industries including adult education, professional services and depository institutions and moat recent as a high school teacher where he was named the Teacher of The Year.

Ydrate's most recent book "Cultivating A Motivated Mindset" and The Poetic Express are available at YdrateNelson.com and Amazon.

Ydrate lives in and travels from Phoenix, Arizona where he resides with his lovely wife Dr. Kendra Stewart Nelson and their 4 kids Eden, Noah, King & Zion.

# YdrateNelson.com

Made in the USA
Middletown, DE
28 March 2022

63304596R00126